Creative Interventions
for <u>Challenging</u>
Children and
Adolescents

186 Techniques, Activities,
Worksheets & Communication Tips
To Change Behaviors

Susan P. Epstein, LCSW, Parenting Coach

Published by
PESI Publishing & Media
PESI, Inc.
3839 White Ave
Eau Claire, WI 54703

Editing: Rebecca Gochanour
Cover: Amy Rubenzer
Layout: Bookmasters & Amy Rubenzer

ISBN: 9781683732471
Printed in the United States of America

PESI
Publishing
& Media
pesipublishing.com

About the Author

Susan P. Epstein, LCSW, has been working with families for over 35 years. A play therapist and family therapist in private practice for two decades, she later launched a coaching business in 2002. As one of the first parenting coaches in the United States, she founded the Parenting Coach Academy, and over the years has trained and certified hundreds of parenting coaches. Between 2009 and 2016, she toured the United States as a PESI presenter, giving over 300 presentations of her cutting-edge seminar, "Explosive, Challenging and Resistant Kids."

Currently, Susan is a boutique business coach working with therapists, coaches, and healers to bring their businesses online. Through mastermind programs, group and individual coaching, as well as multiday live events, hundreds of her clients have moved closer to and realized their professional dreams.

Creative Interventions for Challenging Children & Adolescents is Susan's third published book with PESI Publishing. In 2012, she authored *Over 60 Techniques, Activities & Worksheets for Challenging Children & Adolescents*, followed by *55 Creative Approaches for Challenging & Resistant Children & Adolescents: Techniques, Activities & Worksheets* in 2014. Susan has also self-published five other books geared toward fostering better relationships between parents and their children.

Contents

Acknowledgements

I'd like to dedicate this book to Nathan and Naomi Paulson, my loving parents, my husband Michael and my children Daniel and Sarah for their support and involvement throughout the book writing and editing process.

My father passed away on April 22, 2019 before the publication of this book, at the amazing age of 97. While growing up, my father read poetry to me every night; some serious, but a lot humorous. One of my favorites is Carl Sandburg's poem, "The fog comes on little cat feet." The humorous re-write is, "The frog comes on little flat feet."

Introduction

Over the years, in my various roles as mother, psychotherapist, educator, and parenting coach I have witnessed huge changes in our society in how children and adolescents behave. The issues and problems facing families today are totally different than they were even 10 years ago.

Our kids are exposed to violence on a daily basis through the media and the internet, some experiencing it in their own homes and neighborhoods—including the growing epidemic of school shootings. Kids are struggling with how to manage all of this and remain compassionate and kind. Kids who suffer from mental health disorders and learning difficulties are at higher risk; and kids who grow up in poverty and have all of the above are the real victims.

This book was designed with therapists, teachers, parents, and caregivers in mind to provide easy-to-apply solutions to hundreds of mental health, behavioral, and learning issues facing children and teens today. The activities and tips come from over 30 years of my own work as a play therapist, family therapist, and parenting coach. You will find the worksheets transferable from therapy session to home and to school. This book will be a shared resource for all members of the child/teen's team.

Additionally, you'll also see several guest contributions from parenting experts around the world. The diverse viewpoints and multicultural perspectives they have shared broaden and expand our understanding of children and adolescents world-wide.

Within the book, both clinical and nonclinical areas are covered. I have found that the interventions used on high-risk children and adolescents are easily applied to issues at home that are less intense.

It was in 2012 that I wrote *Over 60 Techniques, Activities & Worksheets for Challenging Children & Adolescents*. Then in 2014, I wrote *55 Creative Approaches for Challenging & Resistant Children & Adolescents*. For this book, I have pulled together the best from both books, added many more cutting-edge and updated tips and strategies, and focused especially on arranging the content so that it's easier to use.

HOW TO USE THIS BOOK

I wrote this book to arm parents and professionals with cutting-edge tips, tools and techniques to open up children's emotional blocks, self-limiting beliefs, and challenges; calm anxiety, worry, and fears; create treatment plans and goal setting; brainstorm next steps for problem solving, strategies for healing, and moving forward; and to encourage bonding, collaboration, and communication.

The first sections are full of therapeutic interventions and activities designed to work on the deeper psychological roots of persistent issues and problems that are not easily solved outside of child play therapy, individual adolescent therapy, and family therapy sessions.

Later sections in the book focus on parenting and other child/adolescent challenging behaviors present at home, school, and in the community. The worksheets are meant to be photocopied so the child/adolescent/parent can write and draw on them, too.

To help you navigate the content, each page is labeled with a usage:

 – Something either the parent or professional does with or guides the child/adolescent to complete.

 – To reinforce learning with a deeper dive into activities or content.

 – An essay or article to give the parent or professional a new perspective on problems or issues.

 – Communication is the cornerstone to a happy, healthy and loving relationship.

Agatha Christie once said, "I like living. I have sometimes been wildly, despairingly, acutely miserable, racked with sorrow, but through it all I still know quite certainly that just to be alive is a grand thing." This quote reminds me of what it is like parenting on the rough days, the days when the kids don't listen, or when a child or adolescent in your life is struggling and suffering. These days are heart-wrenching, and they test parents, teachers, and professionals at the deepest level.

But, even on the very worst days, we wouldn't think of trading in our kids or giving up. We regroup, muster our strength, and show up again. You rally. You reach out for help. You do it because you know your kids need you. You do it because you are their best teachers. You do it because you love them and want them to grow up to be good, kind, productive, loving adults.

Anger & Explosive Behaviors

Attention Deficit Hyperactivity Disorder (ADHD)
Autism Spectrum Disorder (ASD)
Oppositional Defiant Disorder (ODD)
Intermittent Explosive Disorder (IED)

Explosive behaviors are challenging to treat. They have been referred to as being like a "fever." We know the child is suffering but we may not know the cause. Because of this, a thorough assessment and diagnosis is necessary in order to develop a treatment plan that addresses the underlying problem. These problems range from lack of boundaries or learned behaviors ("If I don't get what I want, I'll tantrum.") to severe ASD and the inability to self-regulate one's mood.

In addition, there's a fairly new diagnosis that replaces childhood Bipolar Disorder: Intermittent Explosive Disorder (IED). Explosive eruptions occur suddenly, with little or no warning, and usually last less than 30 minutes. These episodes may occur frequently or be separated by weeks or months of nonaggression. The explosive verbal and behavioral outbursts are out of proportion to the situation, with no thought to consequences, and can include tantrums, tirades, arguments, shouting, shoving, pushing, physical fights, and even threatening and assaulting others.

Most explosive behaviors are preceded by a trigger, which may lead to body sensations such as increased energy, racing thoughts, redness in the face, clenched fists, and in severe cases tremors, palpitations, and chest tightness.

This section provides fun, engaging activities to practice managing frustrations and anger in order to prevent explosive outbursts. Allowing kids to explore what triggers them and providing the tools for immediate calming will give them greater mastery over their emotions.

Sometimes We Lose It

Over the years I've worked with many parents and teachers who ask for help with a child who is out of control. The first meeting is usually like this: "My child doesn't listen," "My child has tantrums," "My child is disrespectful," "My child hit me," and so on.

I ask them about their communication style. "Well, I interrupt my child. I scream and yell. Sometimes I say things I regret and sometimes I lose it." I'll admit that staying calm for adults dealing with challenging kids is hard work. Some kids are difficult a lot of the time, and it takes boatloads of patience not to lose one's cool. Other kids are fine most of the time, and then boom—like a time bomb, they explode: "Why, why, why, can't they just behave?"

Here's why: They are little humans. They have good days and bad days just like all of us. When was the last time that you didn't get frustrated at work, or while being on hold with the insurance company, or while waiting all day for the delivery that never comes, or while waiting by the side of the road for assistance when your vehicle has broken down?

As adults, most of us have learned to modulate our emotions and keep them in check. We have learned not to kick the police officer or scream at the nice tech person we've been on the phone with for two hours while our computer continues to crash.

Sometimes, we even procrastinate, put things off, get distracted—we skip washing our face or brushing our teeth before we go to bed, stay up too late, and break the rules. Sometimes—yes, it's true—we have temper tantrums right in front of our kids!

So the next time your child or the child you are working with has the following behaviors:

- talks back
- whines
- begs
- hits or kicks
- spits or bites
- throws a tantrum
- swears
- threatens to leave, run away, or live with another parent/caregiver
- ignores you or walks away
- throws or breaks things
- intimidates you
- becomes melodramatic
- tries to guilt trip you; and/or
- leaves you out of the loop

Take a deep breath and remember that it is your job to teach them how to act, how to emote, and how to get their needs met. If you are patient and loving and understanding, your child will get it.

It's Not Fair!

Ages: 6-13

Purpose: To untangle what children perceive as fair as opposed to what they want or don't want to do. This activity is especially helpful when working with children struggling with ADD, ASD, ODD, and LDs.

Difficult, challenging and explosive kids believe that the things that happen to them during their day are "unfair." They may have a distorted view of reasonable expectations and demands from parents, teachers, and other authority figures and see these as unfair.

Materials:
- 3×5 index cards
- Pen/pencil/marker

Instructions:

1. Make a set of cards with the following words:
   - *Complete homework*
   - *Do chores*
   - *Go to bed at bedtime*
   - *Take a shower*

2. Add a few hypothetical situations such as:
   - *You are playing cards and your friend takes two turns in a row.*
   - *The teacher passes out cookies, and everyone gets two but you only get one.*

3. Distribute the cards. Ask them the difference between the things they are asked to do and unfair requests.

4. Now ask the child to talk about the things in life that upset them and create a card for each one.

5. Next ask the child to tell you which pile each of their cards belongs in:
   - *Unfair*
   - *Just something I don't want to do*

   After completing step #5, explore with the child why they believe it's either "unfair'" or "just something I don't want to do." The objective is to get "buy in" and then create a plan to expand cooperative behaviors.

Birthday Cake Relaxation

Ages: 5-12

Purpose: To teach young children how to self-regulate emotions, calm themselves and relax.

Instructions:

Read the following script aloud to the child in a calm, slow, and soothing voice. You can also create an MP3 audio recording of the script and email it to the parent for use at home.

Script:

1. Get ready to relax. You can sit in a chair, on the floor, or lie down on a bed.

2. One way to relax your body is by breathing deeply, so you are going to start by focusing on your breathing, and then move into relaxing your muscles.

3. First, close your eyes and pretend you are blowing the candles out on your birthday cake. *Oh, no! The candles won't go out*! Now you are all out of air. Take a big breath in, and blow your candles out again. The candles still won't go out … they are those trick candles … but you keep trying. Breathe in and then blow out the candles … Keep breathing slowly like this. Feel how it relaxes you to breathe deeply. Finally, you are able to blow out all the candles on your cake.

4. Now imagine that your body is like a balloon. When you breathe in, feel your chest and sides expanding, like a balloon filling with air. When you breathe out, imagine your body is like a balloon shrinking with the air being let out.

5. Breathe in like a balloon being blown up. Now breathe out through your mouth, like the air is being slowly let out of a balloon.

6. Breathe in through your nose and imagine your body expanding like a balloon. Now imagine letting the end of the balloon go, and the air rushes out as you breathe out through your mouth.

7. As you breathe in this time, raise your arms above your head. When you breathe out, lower your arms.

8. Breathe in and reach your hands above your head, stretching high up … stretching … and now lower your arms to your sides and relax as you breathe out.

9. Raise your arms and breathe in. Lower your arms and breathe out.

10. Now relax and keep your arms at your sides, while you continue breathing slowly and deeply.

11. Now squeeze your hands closed into fists. Pretend that you are squeezing a lemon in each hand ... gripping tighter ... squeeze even tighter ... squeeze all the juice right out of those lemons. Right now, your muscles are tense.

12. And now let your hands go limp. See how your hands feel relaxed. Notice how "tense" feels different from "relaxed." Relaxation is a way to make your whole body feel at ease like your hands are now.

13. Next, tighten your leg muscles to make both of your legs tense. Pretend you are riding your bike up a very steep hill and you have to squeeze your legs together and utilize all your power to get to the top of the hill. Squeeze tighter ... tighter ...

14. Now let your legs become very relaxed. Each leg is as loose as a piece of string. Your legs feel heavy. The muscles are loose.

15. Now tense your arms. Make the muscles very tight and tense. Tighter ... And now relax so your arms feel limp and loose as pieces of string.

16. Notice how it feels to be relaxed. Your legs and arms are relaxed.

17. Now let your whole body become relaxed. Notice how relaxed you can make your body ... loosening every muscle ... no tension at all ... Your body feels heavy and relaxed.

18. Relax even more by noticing your breathing again. Notice how calm your breathing is. In ... out ... in ... out ...

19. Keep breathing and simply relax. There is nothing you need to do right now except relax quietly.

Calming Cards

Ages: 3-10

Purpose: To help children create images that remind them that they can choose to do an activity to get to a calm and happy place.

Materials:

- 3×5 index cards
- Pen/pencil/markers or crayons
- Glue stick
- Printed images, if desired

Instructions:

1. Ask the child to help you create a list of calm-down strategies specifically for them. One example is the breathing square (instructions below).

2. Then create cards for these calm-down strategies using pictures, words, or both. Some examples are shown below to help you get started.

3. Once you've finished your cards, keep these in the child's "Cool Down Kit" so they can reference them any time they need help calming down.

Breathing Square

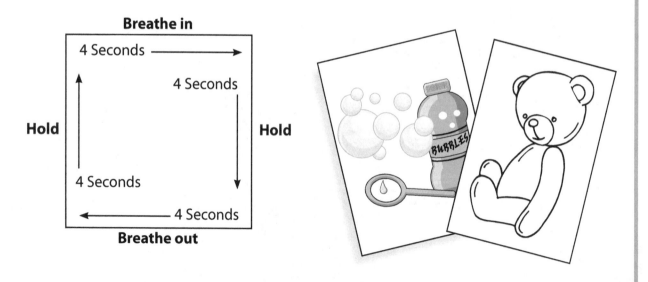

The Feeling GPS

Ages: 4-9

Purpose: To encourage children to monitor their behavior and to help them make a choice about whether or not to let their feelings rule their behaviors. This activity can be used with children and with families.

Materials:

- Copy the image below
- Markers or crayons

Instructions:

1. Guide the child by starting in the center of the map.
2. Ask them to show you with their crayon or marker where their feelings go.
3. Explain to the child that we all "travel" or "move" through feelings, and we get to choose how we feel.
4. Ask the child to show or tell you what they would have to do to go from mad to calm, etc.

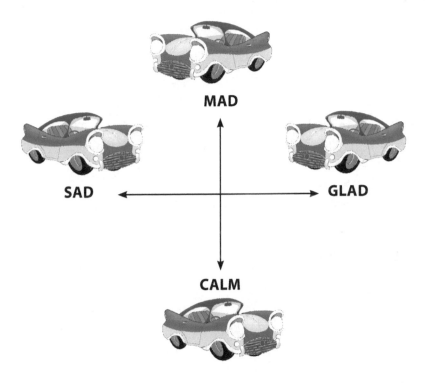

Let's Drive to CALM

Ages: 4-9

Purpose: To help children process the connection between their feelings, their behaviors, and the consequences of those choices.

Instructions:

After you and the child have completed "The Feeling GPS," explain to the child that sometimes feelings trigger kids to hit or take out their feelings on others. For example, when a child goes to the MAD place, they may hit their brother and then their mom may send them to their room. Then ask the child the following, and have them write or draw their answers:

When I go to the MAD place, this happens:

When I go to the SCARED place, this happens:

When I go to the SAD place, this happens:

When I go to the CALM place, this happens:

A Watched Pot Never Boils!

Ages: 4-9

Purpose: To help children monitor and identify feelings. This activity can be used in individual and family therapy.

Instructions:

Helping kids identify their level of anger is the first step in redirecting and managing angry outbursts. Discuss with the child how feelings can be mild, moderate, or intense.

Use the metaphor of a pot on the stove to teach the varying levels of emotions involved in being angry. For example:

1. The "watch" stage: Have the child watch you take a deep breath. Then watch the child do the same.

2. The "steam" stage: This might look like a big sigh or yelling.

3. The "boiling" stage: This stage might involve hitting, shoving, and throwing objects (in other words, a complete meltdown).

4. Showing kids how steam comes before boil is also a great way to teach feeling intensity.

5. Send the activity worksheet (see the following page) home with the parent/caregiver and ask them to monitor meltdowns and explosions for one week.

A Watched Pot

Monitor your child's meltdowns, feelings and the intensity of those feelings for one week and record them below.

Date	Feeling	Watch	Steam	Boils
Feb. 12	MAD	Notice my hands	Screaming	Full-blown temper tantrum

Rag-Doll Relaxation

Ages: 4-9

Purpose: To promote relaxation and self-regulation, and to calm down before bedtime.

Materials:

- The following script
- A small stuffed animal

Instructions:

Read each section of the script slowly, using a calming tone in your voice. As children progress through this technique, they'll pay attention to each muscle group, taking note of the difference between tense muscles and relaxed muscles.

You can also create an MP3 audio recording for parents to use at home.

Script:

1. Lie down on your back and close your eyes. Breathe in deeply through your nose. *[Pause and silently count to three.]* Now let out your breath very slowly, as if you're giving a long sigh: Ahhhhhh. Be aware of the muscles in your face. Relax them, beginning with your jaw. Next, relax your shoulders; feel the tension melt away. Now feel your tummy. Put your stuffed animal on your belly button and hold the stuffed animal in place. Put your other hand on top of that hand. Breathe in deeply and let out the breath slowly. Notice how your stuffed animal rises and falls. Let's make our animal rise and fall 10 times. *[Repeat at least 10 times.]*

2. Next, relax the muscles in your body. Pretend that you have an orange in your right hand. Squeeze as hard as you can and count to five: one, two, three, four, five. Good. Pay attention to the tension in your muscles. Now drop the orange and let your muscles relax. *[Repeat for the left hand.]*

3. Sit up and pretend you're a cat or a dog that's just woken up from a nap. Stretch your arms high above your head. Let your arms drop. Don't try to stop them. Just let them fall. See how good that feels? Now reach for the ceiling. Stretch higher. Higher! Go as high as you can. Now let your arms drop to your side. Doesn't that feel good?

4. Now let's work on your jaw muscles. We're going to pretend that you have a hard piece of candy in your mouth, and you're going to try as hard as you can to bite through it.

Bite hard. Harder! Now relax your jaw muscles. Let's try it again. *[Repeat.]* Relax. Pretend you are swallowing the candy. Yum! Feel the tension melt away in your entire body.

5. We're going to work on your face and nose. Scrunch up your nose as tight as you can, making lots of wrinkles in your face. Just keep scrunching. Now relax. Let's try it again; scrunch harder. Harder! Relax. Notice how relaxed your face feels.

6. Back to your tummy again. You're going to squeeze your belly as hard as you can, making you look as skinny as possible. Now squeeze … squeeze … squeeze. Good. You can relax now. Next, try to make yourself even skinnier and hold it for a good five seconds. Squeeze. *[Slowly count to five.]* Relax. Let's try it one more time. Squeeze as hard as you can. *[Count to five.]* Relax. Now relax your entire body and notice how good that feels.

7. Now, pretend you're on a sandy beach. Use the muscles in your legs and squeeze your toes into the sand as hard as you can. Feel the wet sand squish between your toes. Now relax the muscles in your legs all the way down to your toes. Feel the tension wash away into the ocean. Let's try it again, only this time, dig your toes deeper into the sand, using your legs once again. *[Pause.]* Relax your legs. Relax your toes. Now, relax your entire body.

8. Pretend you're a rag doll, and let your entire body go limp. Notice how good it feels to be relaxed. Now, just enjoy the feeling. I am going to slowly count to three. When I get to three, slowly open your eyes. One, two, three. Do you feel different than you did before we started? *[Let the child answer.]* Tell me what's different about how you feel now. *[Let the child answer.]* Now you know how to melt away the tightness in your body. Whenever you feel worried or upset or scared, take a few minutes to tighten your muscles, then relax them.

Let's Go to the Moon!

Ages: 4-9

Purpose: To teach social skills, such as sharing, taking turns, and working together. Use this activity in group therapy and social skills groups.

Materials:

- Paper
- Markers, crayons

Instructions:

1. Tell the children that we are all going on a trip to the moon. When we land, we will do a fun activity together.

2. Gather the children in a circle and have everyone sit. Count down from 10 until "blast off," when all the children should jump in the air.

3. Announce that we are now on the moon and we are going to make moon memories. Everyone will draw their own picture of the moon, while sharing the markers that are provided.

4. The only way for the group to get off the moon and go home is to share. When one of the children doesn't share, or snatches away a marker from another child, stop the activity and ask the children to talk about how it feels when someone takes something away from them.

You can also get creative here and design trips to other planets or lands to provide variety.

Now You See It, Now You Do It

Ages: 3-9

Purpose: To ease transitions that are difficult for children, to reduce explosive behaviors, and to increase cooperation. This activity is especially helpful for children who struggle with ADD, ASD, ODD, and LDs.

Materials:

- Scissors
- Glue stick
- Poster board
- Clear contact paper
- Pictures (photographs, magazine pictures, images from Google, etc.)
- Yarn or string

Instructions:

1. Use the worksheet on the following page with parents/caregivers to identify the transitions during the child's day.

2. Because young children benefit from visual cues reminding them of what is next, help the child create a string of visual cues for each transition—using the completed worksheet as a guide. You can focus on one or more transitions.

3. Have all of your supplies ready. Every picture should have a label so the child can associate the written text with the picture.

4. Choose pictures for the schedule you wish to create. Keep in mind that a visual schedule is used to assist children with transitions and anticipating activities throughout the day. It can be as specific or as general as the child may need and can be for varying spans of time. For example, a visual schedule may outline parts of a day, a half day, or an entire day. Keep in mind your child's developmental level.*

5. Cut your pictures and poster board squares the same size.

6. Glue the pictures on poster board squares for durability.

7. Punch holes and string the pictures together with yarn or string in the order of the day.

8. Hang from a cabinet or hook at the top of a door.

---

* Tip: Keep in mind the developmental stage of the child. Some children will understand what "getting dressed" means. Others will need a cue for each piece of clothing, such as images for shirt, underwear, pants, socks, and shoes.

Now You See It: Transition Planner

List each transition in the child's day:

1. _____

2. _____

3. _____

4. _____

5. _____

6. _____

7. _____

8. _____

9. _____

10. _____

Now evaluate the following for each transition:

1.   The child needs full supervision and prompting: yes or no

2.   The child needs moderate supervision and prompting: yes or no

3.   The child needs only the visual reminders: yes or no

Once you've collected the information above, create a step-by-step reminder system for the child based on full supervision, moderate supervision and visual reminders. This will allow the adult to help the child complete activities from dressing to chores.

Up, Up and Away

Ages: 3-9

Purpose: To provide children with a mindfulness exercise that will help them let go of problems, annoyances, and irritations; to help children articulate problems that bother them; and to decrease meltdowns and tantrums.

Materials:

- Copies of the hot air balloon coloring page
- Markers or crayons

Instructions:

Work with the child around the triggers that cause them to tantrum or meltdown, using the following as a guide:

1. Ask the child to name problems that upset them, such as someone pushing to the front of the line or someone bumping into them—concentrate on easy-to-let-go-of problems.

2. Give the child an example: "I was waiting in line at the grocery store and the clerk shut the aisle down after I had already put my groceries down. I was so mad! I had to move all my food back into my cart and go to another line!"

3. Brainstorm with the child about things that bug them.

4. Give the child markers/crayons and have them write or draw pictures of each thing/problem on the balloon.

5. Say to the child, "Now let's imagine that the balloon is taking the problem away into space, never to return. How does it feel to watch this problem [insert their words] go up, up and away?"

Tommy the Tiger

Ages: 3-9

Purpose: To help children separate themselves from the problem through storytelling.

Instructions:

The following is an example of a therapist taking a child through narrative storytelling, addressing meltdowns at bedtime. Take the child through a similar question-and-answer format and then assist the child in writing their own letter to the character in their story.

> **Therapist:** If the problem had a name, what would it be?
>
> **Child:** Tommy the Tiger.
>
> **Therapist:** It sounds like Tommy the Tiger shows up right at bedtime and keeps you from going to bed. How does Tommy the Tiger keep you from going to bed? Can you remember a time when Tommy the Tiger didn't show up at bedtime?
>
> **Child:** He doesn't show up on Saturday night.
>
> **Therapist:** What is different about Saturday night?
>
> **Child:** I don't know, it's just different.
>
> **Therapist:** Tell me more about those times. What was different?

[The therapist continues to ask questions and comes up with answers like the following: no homework, lots of time outside to run around, less structure, etc.]

> **Therapist:** What is the worst thing about it when Tommy the Tiger appears?
>
> **Child:** Everyone is mad at me.
>
> **Therapist:** Tell me what it would be like if Tommy the Tiger didn't visit you at bedtime anymore?
>
> **Child:** Mommy and Daddy wouldn't be mad at me.
>
> **Therapist:** What else?
>
> **Child:** I wouldn't be so tired in the morning.
>
> **Therapist:** Great, let's write a letter to Tommy the Tiger and ask him to stay at the zoo and not bother you at bedtime.

Building a Cool-Down Kit

Ages: All

Purpose: To calm down, self-regulate emotions and reduce parent/child conflict.

Materials:

- Bag, shoe box, mini knapsack, plastic container, zip-lock bag, etc.
- All or some of the following: calming cards, crayons, Play-Doh® or Model Magic®, small pad of paper, and relaxation scripts (see "Birthday Cake Relaxation" and "Sailboats on the Sea")

Instructions:

1. Once you have taught the child and parent the different cool-down techniques, celebrate by creating a container for them to be kept in. Depending on the environment, you can help the family create multiple kits for home, school, grandma's, and even day care.

2. The parent or caregiver's role is to prompt the child to use the kit when the child begins to appear agitated. Encourage them to also sit with the child and assist in the cool-down time—so much better than a time-out!

Bonus Tip on Cooling Down with Cotton Balls

Have a cotton ball race with the child: "Who can use the straw to blow their cotton ball across the table/floor first?"

Or . . . use bubbles: "Let's see who can blow the biggest bubble without popping it."

More Ways Parents, Teachers and Professionals Can Support Children's Self-Regulation

In order for a positive change to occur, children need reinforcement in all their environments (especially school and home). Therapists can assist in the process by sharing these supportive questions and statements.

Prompts:

- You seem upset. Would you like your Cool-Down Kit?
- Do you think using the Breathing Square would help you calm down?
- Would you like your calming cards?
- Would you like to play a game or read a book during your free time?
- Remember that if you finish your math problems, you'll be able to go outside for recess with the other kids.

Reinforcing:

- I love the way you are sitting still and eating your dinner.
- That was so nice of you to help your sister with her homework.
- I am so proud of the way you behaved in the supermarket.
- Wow! You stayed in your bed for 30 minutes without getting up!
- Thank you so much for saying "please."

Ending the Explosions

Ages: 13+

Purpose: To teach teens how they can turn habitual negative reactions, situations, and feelings into thoughtful and mindful responses.

Materials:

- Copy the cards on the next page or make your own using card stock (4 pieces) or large sticky notes
- Markers

Instructions:

1. Instruct the teen to decorate four cards with the words:

STOP	**BREATHE**
REFLECT	**CHOOSE**

2. On the back of the **STOP** card, write:
   - What am I feeling?
   - Where am I feeling it in my body?
   - It is okay to feel this feeling.

3. On the back of the **BREATHE** card, write:
   - Breathe in and out slowly five times and notice the breath.
   - Repeat: "I am okay."

4. On the back of the **REFLECT** card, write:
   - How did I react last time?
   - How far back can I remember reacting that way?
   - Who can I turn to for support?

5. On the back of the **CHOOSE** card, write:
   - What are my choices or options?
   - What is my best choice?
   - Choose that now.

6. Go over the questions with the teen and help them brainstorm answers. Add those answers to the cards. Allow teens to keep these cards to remind them that they can choose how to react.

BREATHE	STOP
REFLECT	CHOOSE

My Happy Dance!

Ages: 13+

Purpose: To teach mindfulness and challenge negative thoughts, such as: "I feel sad, but I choose to be happy." Use the following activity with teens during a session.

Instructions:

Brainstorm with the teen some answers for each of the following categories; then create a list of pleasurable activities. When the teen feels sad or unhappy, encourage him or her to take out the list and read it.

People who make me feel happy:

_____

_____

Places I love to go or I would like to visit:

_____

_____

Things I love doing:

_____

_____

Things that make me feel good:

_____

_____

Pleasurable activities I can do:

_____

_____

Agenda Circles:
An End to Power Struggles

Ages: 13+

Purpose: To relieve frustration in the communication between parent and teen.

Materials:

- Copies of the "Agenda Circles" worksheet

Instructions:

Drawing a picture can help both parent and teen see the other person's point of view. Therapists can use the "Agenda Circles" worksheet on the next page to help parents and teens communicate from a place of their own agendas. The parent and teen should each fill out their own circle in the session. After they've done this, bring them through a conversation where both parties get their needs met.

Example:

First Circle: The parent wants the teen to clean up his room.

Second Circle: The teen wants to watch TV.

Third Circle: If Jack makes his bed and picks up his towels, he gets 30 minutes of TV. (Allows for a plan where parent and child can both get what they want.)

Agenda Circles

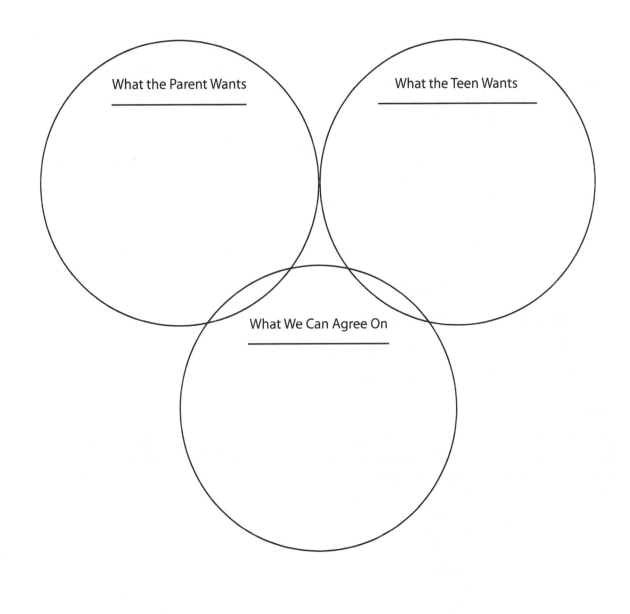

What the Parent Wants
_____

What the Teen Wants
_____

What We Can Agree On
_____

Just the Facts:
Simplifying Communication

Ages: 13+

Purpose: Enhances communication between parent and teen, and gets teens to cooperate without tantrums, meltdowns, and explosions; helps parents remain calm and assertive.

Here's an example of what happens in most homes:

Parent: "I can't believe you left your towel on the bathroom floor again. How many times have I told you to hang it up when you are done? Get in that bathroom right now and hang it up!"

Result:

Teen: "Get off my back! Leave me alone! You pick it up if it is bothering you so much!"

Instead, try using just the facts while remaining calm, clear, and concise:

> "Your towel is on the bathroom floor."
>
> "I feel frustrated because I've asked you to hang it up many times."
>
> "Please hang up the towels when you are done."

Instructions:

Use the "Formula for Just the Facts" worksheet to plan a conversation that you want to have with your teen. (Chores, homework, or a broken agreement are great situations to remove emotions, state the facts, and make a polite request.)

Formula for Just the Facts

State the facts:

_____

_____

_____

_____

Express how you feel:

_____

_____

_____

_____

Make a polite request:

_____

_____

_____

_____

Name It, Don't Blame It!

The next time a discussion with your child or teen starts getting heated, remember to:

1. **Stay calm:** Imagine that you are auditioning to be a robot in a play/movie. You cannot show any emotions during your audition or you will not get the part.

2. **No lectures:** Lectures put kids in the zone of tuning out. All they hear is "blah, blah, blah." They also feel shamed which can lead to explosive outbursts.

3. **No questions:** Questions put kids on the defensive and they feel backed into a corner. This will provoke them to lash out and become angry.

4. **Be clear:** Don't go on and on. Use as few words as possible to make your point. Children/teens will tune out after as few as five words.

5. **Name the behavior:** For example: "Please remove your hand from your hip" or "Please don't roll your eyes. That is disrespectful."

6. **Don't give up until the teen stops:** Every time the teen comes back with another remark, repeat what you just said. For example: "Please don't speak to me that way. It is disrespectful."

7. **Do not banish:** Don't send the child/teen to their room. This sends the signal that you don't care and/or can't deal with them.

8. **Follow:** If the child/teen walks away from you, call them back; and if they still leave, follow while continuing to repeat: "I know you are upset. It's okay to take some time, but please tell me that is what you are doing before you walk away."

9. **Visual reminders:** Use sticky notes, screen savers, etc., to remind yourself to stay calm: "I am a calm parent/teacher and I get results."

10. **Correct with love and guidance:** Show that you care by hanging in there and not losing it, and use "please" and "thank you" when correcting behavior.

Disrespectful Behaviors

Attention Deficit Hyperactivity Disorder (ADHD)
Autism Spectrum Disorder (ASD)
Oppositional Defiant Disorder (ODD)

Adults often unknowingly trigger disrespectful behaviors in kids, especially those with ADHD, ASD, ODD, and LDs. The communication techniques, tips, and worksheets in this section map out the exact steps to have calm, constructive, and collaborative conversations with kids while maintaining a level of authority.

"The Mindful Robotic Tool" is the key to ending backtalk for good. Over the years of practicing as a play therapist, family therapist, and later a parenting coach, the number one reason parents hired me was to help them end the disrespectful behaviors their children and teens exhibited. Kids with the above diagnoses tend to be more disrespectful than other kids.

The tips and activities in this section can be used for all kids, even if there is not a diagnosis. For the professional or parent looking for specific tools to turn disrespectful behaviors around, you will be delighted with how practical and applicable these activities are for kids with mild to severe behavioral issues.

Which Behaviors Do You Want to Stop?

To notice and identify children's negative behaviors so that each can be addressed and turned around. Behaviors that annoy, disrupt, disturb, and are hurtful can show up in many different ways. These can be irritating, and they can also be quite severe and interfere with functioning, relationships, and academics.

Instructions:

Identify behaviors you'd like to STOP by listing them. ("Not listening" is not a "stop" behavior, whereas "ignoring" is.)

List what you want the child/teen to stop doing (e.g., talking back, gesturing, or other disruptive behaviors):

1. _____

_____

2. _____

_____

3. _____

_____

4. _____

_____

5. _____

_____

Parent Activity

Increase Your Parenting Awareness

Purpose: To help caregivers/parents identify where they are in their relationship with their kids, where they would like to be, and help them track their progress.

1. Knowing where you stand and where you'd like to be with your relationship with your kids is the first step. As you go through the "Powerful Parenting Assessment" on the next page, circle the number that reflects where you are today: 0 being the situation at its worst, and 10 being you and your child are doing awesome.

2. After you apply some of the mindfulness exercises and other strategies in this book, go back and retake the assessment. (Clinicians can also use this assessment during the first session of therapy and periodically thereafter to check in with the parent.)

Powerful Parenting Assessment

I don't have patience with my child. I yell and scream, losing my temper.	0 1 2 3 4 5 6 7 8 9 10	I have all the patience in the world; I never lose my temper with my child.
I don't feel respected by my child; my child screams at me, calls me names, and hits me.	0 1 2 3 4 5 6 7 8 9 10	My child completely respects me. When my child is frustrated, we talk it out and move on.
My child does nothing to help around the house; my child leaves a mess in every room.	0 1 2 3 4 5 6 7 8 9 10	My child does chores easily without reminders and pitches in even without being asked.
I dread mealtimes; my child is a picky eater, is never satisfied, and constantly whines that they are hungry.	0 1 2 3 4 5 6 7 8 9 10	I look forward to mealtimes; my child likes to try new things, and we have great conversations.
My child cannot play alone and is constantly begging to play with me. I can't get anything done.	0 1 2 3 4 5 6 7 8 9 10	My child is happy playing alone for extended periods of time. I have time to take care of household chores.
My child won't go to bed, stay in bed, and keeps me up all night long.	0 1 2 3 4 5 6 7 8 9 10	My child goes to bed happily and without a fuss and sleeps through the night.
I dread being at home with my child because it's one power struggle after another.	0 1 2 3 4 5 6 7 8 9 10	I look forward to being at home with my child. Having a child was the best decision I ever made.
I cannot take my child out in public. My child's behavior is out of control.	0 1 2 3 4 5 6 7 8 9 10	I love taking my child out in public. My child is well behaved and listens to my instruction.
I am completely stressed out and exhausted.	0 1 2 3 4 5 6 7 8 9 10	I am well rested and have all the energy in the world.
I am overweight and take lots of medications.	0 1 2 3 4 5 6 7 8 9 10	I am at a healthy weight and take no medications.
I am overwhelmed, sad, and depressed. I have no support.	0 1 2 3 4 5 6 7 8 9 10	I am happy and content and love my life. I have all the support I need.

Commanding Respect

You love your child. You want them to be as great as you know they can be. You want them to grow up healthy with their head on straight. But, somewhere along the line they got "derailed" and started on a path that's led to tremendous stress and anxiety for everyone. Is your child:

- Angry?
- Defiant?
- Disrespectful?
- Unmotivated?

The harder you try to control the situation, the more out of control things get. Maybe they get better for a very brief time (and you hope it will stay this way), but it never lasts, and the next big blowup is always just around the corner.

Case Example

Joey screams at and talks back to his parents all the time. He is constantly picking fights with his younger brothers. He is so angry that his mother, Sharon, is afraid that he is scaring the other children, and she hates to admit it, but she is often afraid of him, too. How horrible, to be afraid of her own son! Mom and dad have gone around and around trying to fix this. They have talked to numerous professionals, tried therapy, and even medications for their son.

Last year, Sharon took Joey to a therapist—more like she dragged him to the appointments. The therapist told her that he doesn't talk and there is not much he can do with him if Joey won't talk in the sessions. The therapist told Sharon to take Joey to a doctor because he might be depressed or bipolar.

Sharon followed the therapist's advice, took Joey to a doctor, and the doctor prescribed three different medications. Sharon had to fight with Joey every day to take the medications. And if that wasn't bad enough, Joey seemed worse. Instead of acting angry, he wouldn't come out of his room. She cancelled the next appointment and stopped giving Joey the medications. Within two weeks Joey started up with the loud, angry outbursts. Living this way was taking a toll on the entire family. Sharon was even noticing that she and her husband were fighting more, and no one in the family was talking to each other. It was like everyone was hiding out!

Many parents find themselves going from therapist to therapist and doctor to doctor with mounting medications and new diagnoses. I've seen this over and over again, and by the time parents met with me, they were at their wits' end and ready to put their child in residential treatment. What had been missing from the treatment was the active involvement of the parent.

They needed to learn a new way of communicating with their child (who may have had ADHD, ASD, or even LDs).

The following tips walk parents through a positive communication process that will reduce and even eliminate angry outbursts, meltdowns, and violence.

1. **Gain Your Child's Attention and Respect**

   Angry kids are not going to cooperate; therefore, YOU must put a stop to backtalk, interrupting, face-making, and other negative body language. Well, you say, "Easier said than done!" Actually, it is simple. The catch is that it takes consistency and a poker face from you. Every time your child engages in one of these negative behaviors, you have to block him or her.

   You ask, "EVERY TIME? ARE YOU CRAZY? How do I do that?"

   Here's the drill: You say to your son or daughter: "Do not speak to me that way." Or "Do not interrupt me." Or "Do not make that face." And the catch is that you have to keep saying it until they stop, while remaining calm all the while.

   Do not let this behavior slide. You need to be ON 100% of the time. So pick a day that you are rested and in fairly good spirits: you'll need to be focused, energetic, and up for a period of continuous effort. Having someone you can call for support if you feel yourself caving is very helpful.

2. **Set Expectations**

   Now that you have your child's attention and respect, let's talk about setting expectations.

   - You do not want your son or daughter hurting or threatening your other children.

   - Spell it out. Tell them directly that this is unacceptable behavior.

   - Then tell them what the consequence will be if this happens.

3. **Consequences**

   It's important that you follow through with the consequence when your children engage in unacceptable behavior.

   A word about consequences: Don't overdo them. Grounding your child for a month will be more of a hardship for you than for your kid. Remember, you will have to see that face day in and day out, begging you to reconsider.

   Think of a consequence that is swift and logical. I personally like community service. An example of this is doing something nice for, or with, the person that you hurt (maybe take over one of their chores or help them with their homework). Doing something for someone else creates an enormous feeling of generosity which, in turn, creates compassion.

Watch Out for Negativity

How do you speak to your child? Do you feel angry and resentful about their behavior? Do you feel that all you focus on is the negative? Then let's try something new: 80% of the time you will focus on your child's strengths—that only leaves 20% negativity. How does that sound?

It is all in the way you phrase it:

- "Is something not going the way it is supposed to?"
- "I know you are trying really hard to control your temper, and I see you catching yourself when you begin to lose it. Is there anything I can do to help you?"

In the second example, you are validating that he is trying, while also offering support and help. This will give him motivation and incentive to try even harder. You can also take the blame off him and put it on the situation. This helps to prevent defensiveness.

Remember, decreasing negativity toward your child has a direct effect on eliciting more positive behaviors!

Overprotection does not mean "not letting him do the things he wants," it means that you are making excuses for his behavior even though he is out of control. Another word for this is *enabling*. If you blame others or the school, you are not being positive toward your child. It means that you are letting him off the hook.

Provide Nurturance and Guidance

Parents everywhere are constantly breaking up fights between siblings. Usually this doesn't turn out very well, with kids and parents losing their tempers. Here's what usually happens:

Parent observes nine-year-old poking his five-year-old brother.

Typical parent response: "Leave your brother alone! Go to your room!!"

The nine-year-old will likely talk back to the parent with "he started it!" and then will probably hit the five-year-old brother even harder a second time.

What if the parent did this instead ...

> **Dad:** Joey, is what you are doing making your brother happy?
>
> **Joey:** No.
>
> **Dad:** Why would you do something to make your brother unhappy?
>
> **Joey:** I'm bored.
>
> **Dad:** Joey, do you enjoy playing with Jason?
>
> **Joey:** Yes.
>
> **Dad:** Jason, do you enjoy playing with Joey?
>
> **Jason:** Yes.
>
> **Dad:** How about we find something you two can play together that you both enjoy?

Let's review this process:

1. Parent demonstrated the skill of problem solving by showing their child how to process a situation and get to a resolution.

2. Parent took command of a potentially hurtful situation by turning it into a teaching moment.

3. Parent asked questions to explore what was truly behind the hitting.

4. Parent turned the situation around by offering an alternative to hitting.

Quick tips to help create compassion and understanding in children:

1. Look for what's really going on.

2. Ask questions.

3. Look for a way to distract from the current situation.

4. Offer to help navigate the process.

Listen for Feelings

It is important to look beyond the words your child is saying, and recognize the feelings they are expressing. Listening for feelings creates a deeper, more loving and trusting connection between you and your child.

Tips:

When interacting with your child:

- What feelings are you noticing? Anger, sadness, disappointment, resentment, jealousy, frustration, happiness, joy?

- Check in with your child about their feelings: "Are you feeling sad or mad?"

- Comment on what you see and ask your child if you are reading them correctly: "I see you are crying and tears are running down your face. That looks like sad to me."

- Validate your child's feelings: "I know you are frustrated that your curfew is 11:00 p.m. Do you want to talk about it?"

- Be open to negotiating if it feels right to you. You will not be spoiling your child. Remember, your child has finally given up the power, and maybe getting something in return will seal the deal. Everybody wins!

- Respond clearly & concisely to your child. For example:

  Joey: Mom, I feel different, everyone else gets to stay out until 11:30 p.m.

  Mom: Joey, I would be willing to do that, but this is what I need from you:

  1. Tell me where you are going.

  2. Call me if you change locations.

  3. Do not arrive even one minute after 11:30 p.m.

Can you do this? And remember Joey, if you are even one minute late you will not go out next Saturday night.

Child and Adolescent Behaviors
That Drive Adults Nuts

Purpose: To assess the seriousness of a teen's out-of-control behaviors that interfere with family and community life. These behaviors can include:

- Talking back/swearing
- Threatening to leave/run away/live with another parent
- Ignoring you/walking away
- Having to repeat yourself over and over
- Inappropriate body language
- Continual cell phone use/texting

Ask the parent(s) to share specific behaviors that are happening at home. Also explore if these same behaviors are happening at school and at other activities that the teen participates in such as religious activities, sports, or visiting a friend's house.

After having this discussion, create a list of the top behaviors that the parent(s) want to stop:

1. _____

   _____

2. _____

   _____

3. _____

   _____

4. _____

   _____

5. _____

   _____

4-Step Process for Calming Down

Purpose: To encourage mindfulness in parents.

Materials:

- 3×5 index cards

Instructions:

1. Create four visual cue cards for yourself:

   STOP   **REFLECT**

   BREATHE   **CHOOSE**

2. On the back of the **STOP** card, write:

   - What am I feeling?
   - Where am I feeling it in my body?
   - It is okay to feel this feeling.

3. On the back of the **BREATHE** card, write:

   - Breathe in and out slowly five times and notice my breath.
   - Repeat: "I am okay."
   - Observe the negative feeling soften.

4. On the back of the **REFLECT** card, write:

   - How have I reacted in the past?
   - How far back can I remember reacting that way?
   - Who can support me here and now?
   - What are my options?

5. On the back of the **CHOOSE** card, write:

   - What are my choices?
   - What is my best choice?
   - Choose that now.

6. Use these cards to assist you in remaining calm and choosing how you want to respond toward your child/teen.

Mindful Robotic Parenting

Purpose: Mindfulness can be a powerful tool for changing emotional reactions and automatic thinking that undermine our parenting effectiveness. Like many other parenting techniques, "Mindful Robotic Parenting" is a practice which becomes stronger and more effective as we repeatedly apply it to our lives.

Instructions:

1. Identify two reaction patterns that you would like to begin changing. For example, becoming angry or impatient with your child.

   a.

   b.

2. List some reasons you think you might have these habitual reaction patterns.

   a.

   b.

   c.

3. List some reasons why you would like to change these reaction patterns.

   a.

   b.

   c.

4. Set a personal reminder to apply the STOP-BREATHE-REFLECT-CHOOSE technique to the two reaction patterns you have identified.

5. Monitor your experiment with this practice:

   • Did you remember to use the four-step process (STOP-BREATHE-REFLECT-CHOOSE)?

   • Was there any change in your reaction?

   • How did the experiment feel?

   • Did you notice any resources that became available to you by applying the mindfulness practice? For example, are you calmer, less reactive, more patient?

Inspiration

Unleash Your Inner Robot

This cheat sheet will prime you to be the calmest parent on the planet. And the best part: it won't feel like work at all. You'll be showing up for your kids, family and the world from a place of inner peace. Get ready to shake things up and have more fun than you've ever experienced raising your kids.

When you connect with your **inner robot**, everything you want for you and your kids is possible . . .

- They start listening

- They start respecting you

- They start cooperating

- And you get more hugs and kisses

Robotic Parenting is your shortcut to peace and harmony at home. Here's a simple seven-step process to rev up your robot and reconnect with the loving, gentle, sweet and kind child you know your child is capable of being:

1. **Chill.** The best robots are relaxed. If you need an idea of how to chill, do one of these: Go for a walk, journal, or meditate before you go any further.

2. **Make a list of everything you want your child/teen to STOP doing** (backtalk, swearing, begging, whining, ignoring, nonverbal gestures). These are all behaviors that, if eliminated, would cause you to be SO in love with your kid that you'd want to squeeze and hug them ALL the time.

3. Bring to mind **your favorite robot,** such as C3PO, R2D2, Rosie from the Jetsons, Robot from *Lost in Space*, or one of your child's toys.

4. **Now imagine that you are that robot.**

5. See that robot responding to a disrespectful comment or demand from your child/teen. **Watch how your robot responds.**

6. Make a decision to **visualize your robot when interacting with your child for the rest of the day.** You should see yourself emotionless in the face of their anger, demands, begging, pleading, swearing, and hitting. You should see yourself calmly repeating one of these phrases:

   - "Please don't speak to me that way. It's disrespectful."

   - "Please don't speak to me that way. It's rude."

   - "Please don't roll your eyes at me."

- "Please take your hand off your hip."

- "Please put your tongue back in your mouth."

7. Go to the computer and **find an image of your robot.**

    - Upload the image to your phone/laptop/tablet and use it as your wallpaper.

    - Print the image and hang it on your fridge, bathroom mirror, the dashboard of your car—multiple places where you will be reminded to stay in your inner robot of calm.

    - Repeat the mantra of your robot: "I am a calm parent who gets respect."

    You've got what it takes to be a robotic parent
    who has respectful, well-behaved, cooperative kids!

Finding Your Inner Robot: A Visualization Exercise

The therapist can read the visualization script to the parent in session or can record an audio file for the parent to listen to at home.

Script:

Begin by getting comfortable. You may want to sit or lie down. Close your eyes or focus your gaze on one spot in the room.

Take in a deep breath through your nose, allowing your belly to expand. When you have filled your lungs with air, blow it all out through your mouth. Continue to do this until you start to feel yourself becoming relaxed and grounded.

Notice your body and if there is tension, tightness, or pain anywhere. Focus on that area of your body while you continue to breathe in and out … now start to send calm, loving energy to that area.

Continue to do this while scanning all the parts of your body. Notice as you focus on each part of your body how relaxed you are becoming.

Now imagine that you are boarding a rocket ship. You are going on a trip to outer space. You buckle yourself into your seat. All systems go. Your rocket ship takes off and you are propelled into outer space. You see the earth becoming smaller and smaller and the swirling galaxy around you. You fall asleep … and when you awaken you find yourself on another planet millions of miles away from Earth.

You look out the window and see a world different from anything you could have imagined … and you are so excited to get out and explore. You open the door to your rocket and step out into this new land. You take in everything around you.

You are approached by a group of friendly robots of different shapes and sizes. Some you recognize from your childhood—from TV shows and video games—and some are completely new to you. The leader approaches you and tells you that he has some sage wisdom to bestow on you:

- *Speak only when you need to.*
- *Keep your sentences brief.*
- *Always be patient.*

- *Be the teacher.*
- *Be the guide.*
- *Listen first.*
- *Then repeat.*

You are completely aware that these robots are superior beings. They are loving, kind, and thoughtful.

One of the robots invites you to step into a special machine where you will be wiped clean of losing control, saying things you don't mean, and all your unnecessary anger, meanness, sarcasm, threats, yelling and screaming, and more.

You enter the machine and a whoosh of air washes over you. You leave the machine feeling lighter, happier, and freer than you have felt your whole life.

Now turn your attention inward … ever more deeply inside … to connect with these new feelings of patience, kindness, love, and guidance.

[Pause]

It will feel good to behave in ways that are consistent with how you want to show up for your kids and other people in your life.

This is the way of the robot.

Now imagine that you are watching yourself as your child begs, screams, rants and raves, hits, kicks, and rolls their eyes at you. Observe how you now react to your child while embracing your inner robot. What are you saying? How are you feeling? See all your anger disappearing … melting away … and notice how your child's anger is disappearing as well.

Your time on this faraway planet has come to an end … as a parting gift, you are handed a package wrapped in beautiful paper and ribbon. You unwrap it, and a huge smile spreads across your face.

Now it's time to say goodbye to your robot friend. You reach out and hug your friend goodbye and thank him for the gifts he has bestowed on you and for his wise words.

You step into your rocket and buckle yourself in for your trip back to Earth. You travel through multiple galaxies and notice how big and vast the universe really is. For a time, you doze off and dream during the long ride back to Earth.

When you land on planet Earth, you step out of your rocket still holding the gift the robot gave you. You are calm and relaxed. You know in your heart that you can always go back to that place and visit.

Spend a few moments now with your gift, remembering all that you experienced and all that you discovered on your journey. Let the wisdom wash over you. Feel a sense of calm and serenity … secure in who you are, knowing who you are. This is your inner robot.

You can take this gift with you in everyday life. Allow it to guide your behavior … to make up who you are and how you respond to others in your world.

[Pause]

It's time to get ready to open your eyes.

Keep your gift close to your heart as you go about the rest of your day.

Wiggle your fingers and toes, waking up your body.

Open your eyes and sit quietly for a moment while you reorient to your surroundings.

You are feeling confident and calm, in touch with your inner robot.

Which Behaviors Do You Want to Start or See More of?

Purpose: Fostering independence starts with identifying the "start" behaviors—behaviors we want to see more of.

Instructions:

List below what you want your child/teen to do. Examples include being on time for school, personal hygiene, completing homework, helping out around the house, etc. Then create an agreement and easy-to-follow steps with you child or teen to help them implement these changes.

1. _____

   _____

2. _____

   _____

3. _____

   _____

4. _____

   _____

5. _____

   _____

Walls: Creating Rules That Make Sense

"Before I built a wall, I'd ask to know what I was walling in or walling out." — Robert Frost

Purpose: To define rules that are logical and reasonable, and that provide a teachable moment.

Instructions:

Use the following questions to clarify the rules you currently have. Then follow up with the worksheet on the next page to help you address the rules that really matter.

Common Questions and Complaints About Kids

Why do you think that your kids won't listen?_____
_____
_____

Why do you think they break your rules?_____
_____
_____

Why do you think they are so disrespectful?_____
_____
_____

Why do you think they are so angry?_____
_____
_____

Questions to Ask Instead

What are you asking them to do that they are choosing to ignore?_____
_____
_____

What is the purpose of the rules you have created?_____
_____
_____

How do you deal with disrespect?_____
_____
_____

Why are you so angry?_____
_____
_____

Before I Build a Wall

If you have a rule, know why. And if you are looking for a place to start, develop rules under these categories:

Ensuring Safety

Example: "No texting while driving."

1. _____

2. _____

3. _____

4. _____

Teaching Manners

Example: "When you want something, use the word *please*."

1. _____

2. _____

3. _____

4. _____

Teaching Consideration

Example: "Call me if you are going to be past your curfew."

1. _____

2. _____

3. _____

4. _____

Take the Gentle Path

Power struggles—we've all been in them; we've started them, and we've been sucked into them. Something so simple becomes a tornado, and it's hard to even remember how we got there.

If you find yourself being pulled into a power struggle with your child, take a deep breath and start a robotic delivery of your expectations:

> *"You will not talk to me that way."*

> OR

> *"It's okay if you don't finish dinner, but the kitchen is closed until 7a.m. tomorrow morning. Your choice."* (And stick with it by repeating this sentence until your kid stops fighting with you.)

Remember, don't let the child see you upset and out of control. Stay calm and take the gentle path.

Go through the worksheet on the next page, "Understanding Power Struggles," to identify what triggers are causing battles at home. Take this one step further by problem-solving each of the areas.

Understanding Power Struggles

Answer the following questions about power struggles you've been a part of.

1. What power struggles do you have?

    _____
    _____
    _____

2. What time of day do these power struggles happen?

    _____
    _____
    _____

3. Who is involved?

    _____
    _____
    _____

4. Are the power struggles around things you want your child to do, or around things you want your child to stop doing?

    _____
    _____
    _____

5. How important is it that one of you wins?

    _____
    _____
    _____

6. How do you feel at the end of the struggle?

    _____
    _____
    _____

Best Friend or Archenemy? What Type of Parent Are You?

Purpose: To learn about your parenting style and to offer an opportunity to have a closer, more rewarding relationship with your children.

Instructions:

If you are having trouble with your kids or are trying to co-parent and it isn't working well, the style of parenting you are using may be the problem. Take the following parent quiz.

Parent Quiz:

Rate the following on a scale of 1 to 3 as to whether it represents your style of parenting:

1. All the time

2. Sometimes

3. Never

1. "My child is my best friend! All her friends love me because I really understand them. They love coming over here because I give them a lot of freedom and space. However, sometimes I wonder if I am too lenient and too permissive." _____

   Note: Parents are usually fearful of their kids. They are afraid to say no because they are afraid that their child won't like them.

2. "My child is my 'archenemy.' He says that he hates me and that I don't get him, and he is either in his room all the time or at a friend's house. I don't know anything about his life. Am I too hard on my child? He is always in trouble with us, and we are all miserable." _____

   Note: Archenemy parents are very strict and often over-punish and over-consequence. They are afraid that their child will grow up and become a really bad person.

Tips for Balanced Parenting

The thing that both types of parents listed above have in common is guilt. Try the following to gain a balanced relationship with your child:

- Forget about being best friends with your child, but do get to know their friends and the parents of their friends.

- Do let your son or daughter have friends over. Give your child space, but be around and aware. Have a set of rules you are both aware of. Make the consequences for failing to obey these rules known.

- Draw up a contract/agreement of what is expected and what will result if the contract is broken.

- Hold your child accountable for disrespectful behavior, and correct them every time you notice those behaviors.

- Remain interested in your child's life, but let them have a life—don't smother them.

And aim for this:

For the most part, I know what is going on in my kid's life.
I know most of his or her friends, and my kid respects most of my rules most of the time.

When to Say "Yes" and When to Say "No"

Purpose: To help you clarify why you respond in a certain way to your children.

Instructions:

When kids ask permission to do something—whether it's to stay up late, play one more game, or not participate in family life—sometimes adults don't think through their responses, setting kids up for tantrums, meltdowns, and chaos.

Use the following to identify situations in which you may not have thought through your response before saying yes or no.

For example:

- *By saying "YES" to staying up past bedtime, I am saying "NO" to a smooth, calm morning.*

- *By saying "NO" to my teen being unsupervised after school, I am saying "YES" to ensuring that my teen won't make risky and unsafe choices.*

Saying "YES" . . . Saying "NO"

1. By saying "YES" to_____ I am saying "NO" to_____.

2. By saying "YES" to_____ I am saying "NO" to_____.

3. By saying "YES" to_____ I am saying "NO" to_____.

4. By saying "YES" to_____ I am saying "NO" to_____.

5. By saying "YES" to_____ I am saying "NO" to_____.

Saying "NO" . . . Saying "YES"

1. By saying "NO" to_____ I am saying "YES" to_____.

2. By saying "NO" to_____ I am saying "YES" to_____.

3. By saying "NO" to_____ I am saying "YES" to_____.

4. By saying "NO" to_____ I am saying "YES" to_____.

5. By saying "NO" to_____ I am saying "YES" to_____.

Inspiration

A Boat Without a Rudder

When parents and caregivers don't provide structure and limits, their children become like boats without rudders at sea.

Many parents and caregivers feel that they can never do enough to please their kids. The more they give, the more their kids beg for more.

As humans, we want to be liked and feel uncomfortable when someone is angry with us or gives us the cold shoulder. We will do anything not to be distanced from, or in conflict with, others. The problem with this and parenting is that it gets messy. Our children's whining and complaining gets to us and wears us down. Then we give in and let them have their way. Once we've fallen into this pattern, it's difficult to find our way out because, in an effort to get their way and to maintain the power, your child becomes even angrier than the last time.

When children become teens, it may seem as if they are closer to their friends than to their own family members, and this can feel hurtful. Remember, you want to be liked, and now they act as if they hate you! Some parents feel that they have to bend over backward to get any attention or to connect with their own kids.

This is where we as parents get into trouble. When parents want kids to like them, they might say "yes" when they really need to say "no," or they might overlook it when their kids say, "Whatever," or roll their eyes. In an effort not to fight or make waves, parents give in over and over again. Remember the old saying, "Give them an inch, and they'll take a mile."

The real truth is that even if it seems that they are disconnecting from you and the family, children need boundaries and rules, and they want you to provide structure and set limits. Kids need direction, and if adults don't provide that, children are like boats without a rudder at sea—drifting along but not going anywhere in particular.

Being a good parent can hurt or feel uncomfortable, but having your kid get in trouble in school or in the community hurts more. Parenting should always be about what's best for the child, whether or not the child realizes it at that moment. Isn't that true love and caring?

Inspiration

Meta-View

Visual reminders help parents and caregivers to stay calm when dealing with kids' challenging behaviors.

Although my kids are grown, they are still my "kids." When we get together, it's funny how I see some of the same behaviors, traits, and interactions that were present when they were children. I am watching this all from a meta-view and am super conscious of my triggers and reactions.

I am continually reminded of my own part in our relationship and that they are their own people with their own lives.

Kahil Gibran wrote about children in his book *The Prophet*, "They come from you but they are not you."

When children are frustrated, angry, disrespectful, or shutdown, your first impulse may be to snap. As a parent, you may think that their behavior is a personal affront against you. This is completely not true. Their backtalk, reactions, and meltdowns are their own inability to process what's going on in a given moment. Here's how you can help:

- Listen.
- Watch for your triggers.
- Correct with love and guidance.
- Treat your children with the respect that you would like from them.

Take some time to come up with a list of simple reminders to help you stay calm, and remain nonreactive. For example "I am a calm parent;" use my robot voice; "breathe." Then transfer that list to sticky notes, screen savers, and personal notes to keep you focused on how you are showing up and interacting with the kids in your life.

Great Job!
Breaking Away from Negativity

Children are often awarded negative attention, getting scolded for doing things they shouldn't be doing, such as:

"Stop hitting your brother!"

"You are so rude!"

"Learn some manners!"

This approach often backfires and turns into huge battles of the will.

Instead of correcting through lecturing, start by noticing and complimenting kids whenever they do something right or comply with your request. For example:

Mom: Mary, please turn off the TV now and come to dinner.

Mary: Okay, Mom.

> Mary *turns off the TV and goes to the dinner table.*

Mom: Thank you, Mary. I really love it when you listen to me the first time. Great job!

Additionally, take notice whenever your child does a chore or something else required. For example:

Teacher: Josh, you've been able to sit still today and complete your math problems. Great job!

Random Acts of Kindness Wall

Purpose: To encourage empathy, compassion, and good deeds at home (and school!). By focusing children's attention on the type of behavior you want from them, you will notice a decrease in the type of behavior you want less of!

Materials:

- Space on a wall or a big bulletin board
- Pens, pencils, and/or markers
- Several photocopies of doves or happy faces
- Pushpins and/or tape

Instructions:

1. Make 5 to 10 copies of the images below, and then let the child/children cut out the images for the "Random Acts of Kindness Wall."

2. Tell the child that whenever they notice someone in the family or in the group doing something for another person or being kind, they are to take one of the cutouts and write the other person's name on it and the nice deed they did. For example: Susie helped Sarah pick up her backpack when it fell off the chair.

3. Then have them tape or pin the cutout to the Kindness Wall for all to see.

4. Have a Random Acts of Kindness Week or Month and challenge the kids to see how many cutouts they can put on the wall. At the end of the event, celebrate by reading all the cutouts aloud and have a little party with surprises and treats to celebrate all the kindness in your home or classroom.

Teaching Your Kids How to Really Say "I'm Sorry"

To encourage kids to apologize in a meaningful and heartfelt way, try using this three-step process to help your child acknowledge or admit what they did, connect to why what they did was wrong, and identify what they should do differently in the future. This process helps children become more emotionally intelligent and empathetic, while developing problem-solving skills. It also helps them to build better relationships.

Three-Step Apology Process:

1. *"I'm sorry for … "* Here is where they acknowledge what they actually did that was wrong or hurtful.

2. *"It was wrong because… "* This step helps them to think deeper about why what they did was wrong or hurtful to the other person.

3. *"Next time I will … "* Having them think about what they will do differently in the future helps them to acknowledge that no one's perfect, and that they may encounter the situation again, as well as what they can possibly do differently next time. This helps them to become both forward thinkers and solution finders.

While working through the three-step apology, here are a few helpful do's and don'ts:

Do …

*   Make them repeat themselves until they can say it in a respectful tone (without making faces). Sometimes step 1 may get repeated several times, but step 2 and 3 go much easier this way. This is important so they learn that how we say something is just as important as what is being said!

*   Give them the prompts to follow, having them repeat it fully and then answer. This is an important step because it engages their responsibility.

*   Thank them and acknowledge when they complete the steps.

*   You may want to take note of their solutions from step 3 and offer those up when/if the situation comes up again.

Don't …

*   Force them to do this in the heat of the moment. Take some time to have all involved calm down.

- Jump in with the answers. Give them time to think about their responses, and after they answer you can respond and help them to be more compassionate or find more solutions if needed.
- Expect it to be perfect the first few times. Consistent (and persistent) use helps this process to become easy, natural, and meaningful. Give it time to work.

After using these steps several times, and depending on the age and learning style of the child, it may be helpful to give them the worksheet on the following page to work on by themselves.

By Sandy Hall, Parenting Coach

"Pleeeeease, You Promised!" The Art of Blocking and Affirming

We often knee-jerk react to our kids' negative behaviors and within a split second our homes and classrooms turn into a battleground. An hour later, we are kicking ourselves, wondering why we didn't act calmly and use our robot voices.

Every parent/caregiver wants to make sure their kid gets it—whatever the "it" of the day is. Here are some common ways adults try to get their point across:

- Explaining the same thing again and again: *"No, you can't have a cell phone. You are not old enough, and it's too much money, and you'll probably lose it … blah … blah … blah …"*

- Lecturing: *"Don't keep asking me for the cell phone. I told you the reasons why. You are getting on my nerves, and I need some peace and quiet around here."*

- Questioning: *"How many times have I told you 'no' about the cell phone? I'm not discussing it anymore. How come you don't get 'no' when I say 'no'?"*

- Negotiating: *"Maybe if you are good all weekend, I'll think about it."*

- Yelling: *"I told you not to bring that up again!"*

- Ignoring: Shutting down and not speaking to the child.

- Sending away: *"Go to your room!"*

Kids know what our automatic responses will be, and they are overly prepared for the comeback:

- Begging: *"Pleeeeeease!"*

- Challenging: *"You promised!"*

- Crying: *"Everyone else has one."*

- Tuning out: *"La, da, la, da."*

- Guilt: *"I hate you! You're so mean!"*

The following are approaches that work for affirming:

- Robotic approaches: Repeat, *"This is not up for discussion,"* calmly until your child stops.

- Listen and affirm: *"I know that this is important to you, but the answer is no."*

- Follow: If your child walks away, follow them, get them to look at you, and then say, *"Do not walk away from me. It is disrespectful."*

- Don't send them away and don't leave: Stick it out. Sending your child away or leaving them feels like rejection and banishment to a kid. Stay with your child until they stop.

It does take a bit of energy up front to put on the calm face. But in the long run, you will save energy and avoid power struggles, tantrums, meltdowns, and slammed doors.

Choices: Getting What I Really Want

Ages: 5-9

Purpose: To help children make choices that give them the outcome that they truly want.

Instructions:

Use this exercise to encourage children to see how their behavior sometimes gets them the complete opposite of what they want.

1. Use the worksheet on the following page with the child to help them understand how their choices affect the outcome of what happens.

2. Then offer the child help in getting what they want by problem solving and brainstorming ways that don't result in negative behaviors and in consequences that they don't like or want.

Here is an example of a boy who regularly hits his brother and is sent to his room:

Parent: Do you like being sent to your room?

Child: No!

Parent: If you didn't hit your brother, would you be sent to your room?

Child: Nope.

Parent: Why do you hit your brother?

Child: I want him to play with me.

Parent: When you hit your brother, does he play with you?

Child: No, I get in trouble.

Parent: Right. And you get sent to your room.

Child: Yes.

Parent: Would you like me to help you get to play with your brother and not get sent to your room?

Child: Yes!

Choices: Getting What I Want

The negative behavior was:

_____

_____

_____

_____

The outcome of the behavior was:

_____

_____

_____

_____

Is the child happy with the result?

_____

_____

_____

_____

What did the child want before exhibiting the negative behavior?

_____

_____

_____

_____

Pay the Jar

Ages: 5-9

Purpose: To reduce sibling conflict, hitting, kicking, name-calling, and other unwanted and challenging behaviors at home.

Materials:

- Glass jar
- Labels
- Coins

Instructions:

1. Label a jar with the word "FINES."

2. Give the kids each $2 in quarters at the beginning of the week.

3. When the child hits, kicks, or name-calls their sibling they must pay the jar. (For example: 25 cents for a name, 50 cents for a smack, etc.)

4. If they keep their language "appropriate" and keep their hands and feet to themselves, they can keep the coins.

Miss-Takes! New Takes!

Ages: 5-9

Purpose: Mistakes are a part of life, and teaching children to handle them in positive ways encourages them to take personal responsibility and provides a great opportunity for them to learn.

Instructions:

Think of a mistake as a miss-take! You interpreted the situation incorrectly, and you made a choice to do something or behave in a certain way.

Using the following three steps, work with your child to change their miss-takes into new takes.

New Takes!

1. See it: "I made a mistake."

2. Say it: "I'm sorry."

3. Solve it: "Let's work on a solution together."

The first two steps— "See it" and "Say it"—encourage mindfulness and connection. The third step teaches learning through making a mistake, and focuses on the teachable moment rather than the typical "shaming." It is crucial to go through all three in this order for the teachable moment and to lock in the learning.

Trauma & Depression

Post-Traumatic Stress Disorder (PTSD)
Difficult Situational Adjustments

The activities in this section focus on giving words to difficult situations, and engaging kids who are silent by using nonverbal techniques to create trust and safety.

Communicating with kids who won't talk can be frustrating and challenging. A nonverbal session is uncomfortable for the therapist and it's natural and understandable that firing questions or talking nonstop to end the silence might occur. Ironically, this is the worst thing we can do because kids will automatically shut us down and dig deeper into silence.

Establishing rapport with the child is the first step in establishing a trusting connection and might include positioning yourself to their eye level, following their lead, and allowing them to choose what to play with.

Over the years, I've created multiple activities and tools that are fun and easy to use in therapy sessions or in the classroom. Some kids will never open up and talk, but that doesn't mean that they aren't connecting with you and getting support, compassion, and healing. Being with another human being who truly cares can be the most transformative treatment of all. An example of this is "Sand Tray Therapy" which is done in almost complete silence.

Outer Space —
Seeing the Big Picture

Age: 5-9

Purpose: To encourage children to pull back and see their problems from the meta-view rather than being caught up in the small stuff. This is especially helpful for kids with OCD (Obsessive Compulsive Disorder).

Instructions:

Tell the child that you are going on a trip into outer space. Ask them to close their eyes and then read the following script to the child.

Script:

Please fasten your seatbelt and get ready for a trip to outer space. In a few moments, we are going to take off and travel way into outer space. OK, here we go, get ready: 10, 9, 8, 7, 6, 5, 4, 3, 2, 1—blast off!

We are traveling fast. As you look out your window you can see your house, now your street, now your city, and now your state. Now you can see water and the coastline. We just broke through the clouds and now we are flying through the solar system and beyond.

Let's float here for a while and look at all the pretty stars, and look—there is planet Earth.

Take out your special binoculars to look down from outer space and see us in this room. We are going to look at your problem from way up here.

What do you notice? How tiny are you? Me? The universe is so big. Let's talk about your problem from up here. What can you tell yourself about your problem when viewing it at this distance?

What Would the Lamp Say?

Ages: 12+

Purpose: To elicit multiple, diverse perspectives in teens, making problem solving fun and creative. Use this activity when you have worked with the teen on coping strategies to help improve a situation, but nothing seems to be working and the teen is becoming more frustrated (for example, if a teen says, "I have no friends.").

Materials:

- Paper, pen or pencil

Instructions:

1. Ask the teen to look around the room and name at least 10 objects, such as a lamp, desk, book, mug, calendar, and so on.

2. Write these down as the teen dictates.

3. Now ask the teen to share what each of these objects would say about the problem or issue. It has to be from the perspective of that object using metaphor. If the teen has difficulty understanding the concept, offer a few examples to model the exercise.

    For example:

    The lamp says, "We have to shed more light on the problem."

    The book says, "We need more information; keep looking deeper."

    The calendar says, "Let's look at how long you've had this problem."

It Looks Like Fun!

Ages: 4-9

Purpose: To help interaction with the child who won't play or engage with you.

Materials:

- Paper
- Markers, crayons, or colored pencils

Instructions:

1. Get out a piece of paper and start to draw a picture by yourself.

2. Lean over the picture to hide your work. Children are naturally curious and the child will most likely try to see what you are doing.

3. Don't let the child see what you are doing at first.

4. As they approach (and they will, as children are naturally curious) say tentatively, "Okay … you can watch."

5. Continue drawing for a few more minutes.

6. Hand a crayon or marker, and encourage them to draw with you.

7. As the child moves in closer, ask the child if they would like to help you finish the picture.

Big Bird Grows Up

Ages: 8+

Purpose: To connect with a resistant, non-talkative or selective-mute child. Therapists and teachers can find themselves standing on their heads to get kids to open up and communicate. I developed this technique when working with a selective-mute nine-year-old girl.

Materials:

- Yellow sticky notes
- Pens

Instructions:

1. Start a conversation on a sticky note. Write "How are you?" Then stick the note on the child's arm.

2. Hand the sticky notes to the child. Give the child the pen and say, "Write your answer on the note."

3. They will answer your question and then stick the note on you.

4. Keep going back and forth and see how many sticky notes you can generate. Usually this will create some giggles as the sticky notes cover your bodies and you both begin to resemble *Sesame Street's* Big Bird.

Beautiful Bags

Ages: 5-13

Purpose: Engaging with a resistant or non-talkative child or teen in a structured, fun, non-threatening way. This exercise teaches children and teens that therapy can be fun and purposeful, while taking the heaviness out of the therapy session.

Materials:

- Paper bag
- Stickers, glitter, glue stick, etc.
- Markers
- Sticky notes or small pieces of paper
- Timer

Instructions:

1. Session #1: Give the child the craft supplies and the paper bag and say: "Today you get to just create. This is your bag to decorate. I'll tell you later how we are going to use this in our work together." (The therapist keeps the bag at the end of the session.)

2. Session #2: Explain that you and the child are going to play a game using a timer. Possible ideas include:

    "In the next 60 seconds, I want you to say as fast as you can all the things that upset you, no matter what they are." As the child starts naming these, write each one on a sticky note or small piece of paper and throw it into the bag.

    "In the next 60 seconds, I want you to say as fast as you can all the different worries or fears that you have." As the child starts naming these, write each one on a sticky note or small piece of paper and throw it into the bag.

3. Session #3: Instruct the child to close their eyes and pull out one of the slips of paper. This will be what you talk about that session. If the child doesn't want to talk about that one, have them put it back in the bag and select another.

4. Each week, another slip is pulled out until all the issues are discussed and the bag is empty.

    Some kids will respond to some of the slips of paper with: "I'm good with that now, but I want to talk about this instead." Abandoning the bag is okay, it was just used to get started. Other kids will ask if they can add more to the bag; also okay!

Blue, Blue

Ages: 3-9

Purpose: To help young children express feelings. Putting words and colors to feelings helps foster appropriate expression of emotions. This can be used in play therapy with young children, or taught to parents for use at home to encourage positive emotional expression.

Materials:

- Three crayons or markers:

    Blue = sad

    Red = mad

    Yellow = glad

- Pad of paper
- Jar or basket

Instructions:

1. Teach children the association between the color and the feeling:
    "Blue is sad: People say they feel blue when they are sad."
    "Red is mad: Cartoon characters turn red when they get mad."
    "Yellow is glad: We are so glad when the sun comes out and it makes us smile."

2. Keep the three crayons/markers and paper in the jar/basket in an easily accessible place in the child's home.

3. When they act out, or want to express themselves, ask the child to make a picture: "Show me how you are feeling with the colors."

4. For younger kids, hold the crayons and ask them to point to the one that they are currently feeling. Then ask them to make a picture with that crayon.

5. After school is also a great time to use this: "Show me with the colors how much sad, mad, and glad you had today at school."

Nightmares and Superheroes

Ages: 3-9

Purpose: To help children who have disturbing dreams and sometimes have difficulty falling back to sleep take control of their fear and sleep through the night.

Materials:

- Paper
- Markers
- Crayons
- Glitter

Instructions:

1. Ask the child to tell you about the dream/nightmare.

2. Ask the child to draw a picture of the nightmare.

3. Now tell the child to tear up the drawing.

4. Ask them to create an alternate ending to the nightmare or to create a superhero to come in and save the day.

5. Have the child draw a picture of the "new dream."

6. Discuss how this new dream is going to protect them from the scary nightmare.

7. Have the child hang the picture above their bed and talk about it before bedtime.

Bad Things Happen to Great Kids

Ages: 5-12

Purpose: To reduce the stigma of trauma with the reminder and knowledge that other kids have had similar experiences. By rearranging the list from bad to worse, kids gain a sense of control, power, and hope.

Materials:

- Paper
- Pen/pencil
- Scissors

Instructions:

1. Explain to the child that you are going to make a list together of all the terrible things that can happen to children. Take turns saying these things out loud while the adult (therapist/parent) creates the list (if the child is a non-reader pictures can be drawn).

2. Some things that could come up include:

   - Being teased/bullied

   - Parent dying

   - Parent in jail

   - Sexual/physical abuse

   - Being abandoned

   - Throw some outrageous ones in too, such as "being eaten by a lion."

3. Now ask the child to cut the paper into strips so that each statement is its own piece of paper.

4. Instruct the child to put the strips in order from bad to worse.

5. Then discuss the order with the child, sorting out the inconsistencies and discussing the reasons the child ordered them in that particular way.

I Am

Ages: 9+

Purpose: To increase feelings of self-worth and confidence in children who are depressed, anxious, or worried.

Materials:

- Play-Doh or modeling clay
- Paper
- Pen

Instructions:

1. Brainstorm several positive attributes with the child. For example: brave, a good friend, artistic, good speller, organized, etc.

    I am _____.

    I am _____.

    I am _____.

    I am _____.

    I am _____.

2. Provide the child with an assortment of different colors of clay or Play-Doh.

3. Tell the child to pick one thing from the list and create an image out of the clay/Play-Doh to represent it.

4. After the child makes the clay image, ask them, "Why did you choose that one? What can you tell me about it?"

5. Encourage the child to choose another attribute from the list and to do the exercise again. Have the child take the images home to reinforce positive thoughts and to increase self-worth.

Helping Children Grieve

Purpose: Processing your own childhood experiences with death in order to help your children express their emotions regarding death.

Instructions:

Coping with a death in the family is one of the most difficult challenges that children will experience. Whether it is a parent, grandparent, or pet, kids need the ability to express their emotions. Before you begin explaining death to a child, it may be very helpful to look back at your own childhood experiences with death. Take time to think through the following questions:

Did anyone talk to you about death?

_____

_____

_____

What did they tell you about death?

_____

_____

_____

Do you have stories or experiences with death that you have never spoken about?

_____

_____

_____

Do you remember what you were told about what happens when someone dies?

_____

_____

_____

Parent FAQs About Children and Grief

Because of their own past experiences and fears, some parents may think they need to protect their children from dealing with death. Most parents are fairly confused and turn to professionals for assistance. This handout provides answers to frequently asked questions parents/caregivers have when talking with their child about death.

1. **How do I explain death to a young child?**

   Tell your child the truth and answer your child's questions: "Grandma was sick and her body didn't work anymore," or "John's dad was killed in a car crash." Go to the library and check out children's books on death and read them to your child.

2. **What words should I use to describe death to my child?**

   Use language they can understand. Be careful not to use the words "went away," "passed," "lost," etc. Young children will take you very literally and want to know why the loved one has not returned or will want to go look for them.

3. **How much information should I share with my child?**

   Use common sense for how much information you need to share based on the developmental stage of your child. Keep it simple. For example, "Grandpa got sick and his heart stopped working. When someone is very old, their heart isn't as strong."

4. **Should I bring my child to the funeral or service?**

   If your child can sit through a service without you having to entertain them or having to get up and take them out, they can go to the funeral. Being with family members is natural. Seeing people cry at a service is normal, too. It is okay for your child to see this. "Everyone is very sad, and they will miss Grandpa very much, that is why they are crying."

5. **Should I let my child see me cry?**

   Yes. Grieve in front of your child. Do not hide your sadness. Instead, show it is okay to cry when someone dies. Also, demonstrate how you can deal with your sadness. Together with your child look at pictures of happier times with the loved one who has just died and ask your child to draw a picture of a favorite time with that person.

6. **What should I say when my child sees me sad?**

   Your child will ask you if you are sad. Answer simply, "Yes, I am sad because I loved Grandpa very much and I will miss him."

7. **How do I keep the memories alive of the loved one who has died?**

   Talk with your child about the experiences that they had with the loved one. Look at photos together and make it okay to bring up the loved one's name.

8. **What if my child thinks that I will also soon die?**

   Explain to your child that this is not likely—but be careful: "We all will die. We just don't know when. Most people live a long life."

9. **How do I know if my child is grieving in the "right way"?**

   There is no right way to grieve. Every child will grieve differently. And there is no length of time when your child should be "done" or "over it." It is a process, and grief needs to run its course. Sometimes parents are so overwhelmed themselves in grieving that they would benefit from some help and guidance from a therapist or support group.

Inspiration

Obesity and Depression: The New Childhood Disease

Overweight children, compared to children with a healthy weight, suffer more from social discrimination and low self-esteem. Depression in children and adolescents can be the cause and the consequence of obesity. In fact, some kids who are overweight have a higher level of anxiety than do other children.

The fallout from this includes things like these:

- Teasing at school and through social media.
- Difficulties playing sports, which compounds the problem.
- Fatigue, which contributes to depression.
- Sleep apnea, which contributes to poor sleep and thus a shorter fuse.

Our hearts break for these kids, and we oftentimes don't know how to help.

What can we do to help?

- Let the child know he or she is loved and appreciated.
- Have a medical evaluation completed first to rule out a physical cause.
- Emphasize healthy eating—clean out your cabinets together and read the labels.
  - Create awareness by making three piles on the kitchen table: foods to keep, foods to never buy again, and foods to throw away (look for sugar and other unhealthy additives).
  - Shop together for fruits, vegetables, and lean protein.
  - Plan meals and cook together.
- If you suffer from being overweight or obese yourself, create a family goal to get healthy.
- Take walks together and plan active outings.
- Be a role model so your child has someone to look up to and admire.

Inspiration

You Are What You Eat

Many factors go into raising a well-behaved, respectful, and happy teenager. But one that can make a huge difference all on its own is your teen's diet. We all know the difference between healthy and unhealthy food, but how many of us actually stick to a truly healthy diet, and furthermore, help our kids do so too?

In the late 90's, a small company in Wisconsin called Natural Ovens initiated a five-year project to bring healthy food into area schools. The goal was to show that fresh, nutritious food can make a real difference in the student's behavior, learning, and health.

Instead of vending machines full of sugary sodas and snacks, only water and fruit juices were sold. Instead of frozen boxes of food being shipped in, fruits, vegetables, grains, and lean meats were prepared fresh for the students. The results were amazing.

What was once a school ridden with dropouts, expulsions, drug use and kids carrying weapons, has now done a complete 180. Mary Bruyette, a teacher at the school said, "Our biggest problems now at the school are parking in the parking lot and student tardiness. I don't have the disruptions in class or the difficulties with student behavior that I experienced before we started the food program."

While there might not be great lunch programs in your children's schools, you still have control over what they eat at home. A healthy diet is one great way you can help your kids be healthier as well as better behaved.

By Daniel Rosenkrantz

Autism Spectrum Disorder (ASD) & Related Issues

Autism doesn't impact all kids in the same way, and some kids with autism have a lot in common with kids with learning and attention issues. To some degree, that's because the symptoms overlap. For example, kids with autism may show some of the following traits:

- Issues recognizing others' feelings and reading nonverbal cues. This presents when kids interpret idioms literally, and misinterpret humor and common sayings. "Hold your horses," for example, could illicit, "I don't have any horses!" These symptoms are also seen with social communication disorder, ADHD, and receptive language issues.
- Difficulty with executive function. Some kids with autism find it hard to get organized and solve problems. They struggle to regulate their emotions. Even a slight change in a routine could trigger an outburst. Kids with ADHD and Executive Functioning Disorder often have similar issues.
- Seeking out or avoiding sensory input. This is also common in kids with sensory processing issues and ADHD.
- Clumsy and uncoordinated. Kids may have trouble with handwriting, riding a bike, catching a ball, or running. These can also be symptoms of dyspraxia, dysgraphia, and sensory processing issues.
- Trouble working with words. Many kids may struggle to express themselves coherently, follow conversations, and speak with appropriate volume and inflection. These are also symptoms of speech-language issues and nonverbal learning disabilities.

Because of these similarities, it may seem like both groups of kids would benefit from the same type of interventions. But there are differences between learning and attention issues and autism that are important to understand.

When kids are misdiagnosed at a young age, it creates various problems for them and their families. Diagnoses overlap, and treatment planning should reflect the whole child. Knowing what's really wrong and being able to navigate the complex system of school, community, and mental health is the key to a child's overall health and well-being.

Inspiration

What's Really Wrong?

Children don't live in their own apartments; they live with their families. That's why it's so important that all the helping adults involved try to understand what impact a "bad" kid's behavior has on their family. Teacher, therapist, and parent all want the same outcome for the child: to be successful and confident. How each adult perceives or addresses the situation will probably be very different.

Many parents have noticed the following signals:

- Child has difficulty learning

- Child's behavior at home and at school is extremely difficult to manage

- Child has had numerous suspensions

Parents may have asked themselves the following questions:

- Is my child's behavior just a phase?

- Can my child's school help us?

- Should my child see a professional? Which kind of professional?

    – And what can they do?

    – How do I find a good one?

- What other services are out there?

- Does my child already have an Individualized Education Program (IEP) and/or is my child on medications like Ritalin, Adderall, and other stimulants with little or no effect?

- Has the school not implemented or followed through with my child's approved program, and is my child becoming more depressed and out of control?

- Has my child begun to isolate from friends and family? Is my child smoking marijuana or drinking? Or might they be engaged in other risky antisocial behavior? Or are they already involved in the juvenile justice system?

Tips for getting started:

1.   Don't wait to take action.

    - Don't think a child will grow out of their difficulties.

    - Don't wait until the end of the next semester to revisit the issue.

    - Three months, six months, or one year is a significant amount of time to let pass in a child's education.

2. Meet with the child's teacher immediately.

   - Do not wait for parent-teacher conferences to raise concerns.

   - Don't accept the teacher's recommendations to wait until the end of the semester, or that the child will grow out of it.

3. Have the child's vision and hearing screened.

   - Often, a child's learning difficulties can be caused by a hearing or visual impairment.

4. Request an evaluation.

   - Schools will provide an "Initial Psychological-Educational Evaluation" at their expense, which can give a baseline on your child's cognitive ability, academic achievement, and emotional health.

5. Schedule a neuropsychological evaluation.

   - Check with your pediatrician to get a referral. There is often a long wait for an appointment.

By Mindy Mazur, MPH, Educational Therapist

Informed, Involved, and On Board

Children experience the best outcome if there is a treatment team made up of parents, family members, teachers, therapists, and physicians.

Children and adolescents are being diagnosed with mental health disorders that may lead to or require psychotropic medications. These diagnoses include ADD (Attention Deficit Disorder), ADHD (Attention Deficit Hyperactivity Disorder), Bipolar Disorder, and ODD (Oppositional Defiant Disorder).

Nine-year-old Jenny often interrupts, doesn't listen, doesn't complete tasks, is often obstinate, and treats authority figures with little or no respect. At home, parents yell, scream, ground, and then do it all over again.

It seems like 11-year-old Bobby has come off one grounding only to find himself grounded again. Mom feels like a prison guard and the home is hostile and tense. At school, the story repeats.

Johnny is the class clown, constantly talks back to the teacher, and serves detention after detention. At the parent-teacher conference the teacher recommends that Johnny get tested for "ADHD or other issues." The parent may be relieved—at least his negative behavior has a name! Life is finally going to improve! A psychosocial evaluation is recommended and carried out by the school: now Johnny has a diagnosis. Sometimes, however, this very important step is skipped.

Most state school systems are not permitted to recommend medication. However, they can say, "Talk to your pediatrician," or "Your child needs counseling." Most parents, when given such feedback, will take their child to the pediatrician who will often prescribe medication or make a referral to a psychiatrist. There is no blame here; the system is clogged with kids like these, and teachers and pediatricians are overworked and often not equipped to spend more than a few minutes with parents directing them on next steps.

Behaviors don't change with only the medicine, so the psychiatrist refers the child to a psychotherapist. The most common form of therapy is individual play therapy for children and individual therapy for adolescents.

In the beginning, parents will likely see some positive changes in their child's attitude and behavior and begin to see some progress at home. The child may seek out his parents more or even treat them respectfully once in a while. We call this the honeymoon period. The parent is driving the child to therapy, the child is playing or talking with another adult who cares about them, the parent is driving the child home from the therapy appointment. By nurturing the child and spending alone time with them, they will naturally respond to this positive attention and their behavior will improve.

Then it's over. The child is suspended again for getting in a fight, or pushes his mother, or doesn't come home for three days.

What went wrong?

When we medicate a child for behavioral problems and refer them to individual therapy, we may be doing a disservice to the child. When children and adolescents are treated in the context of the family and all are on board, the outcomes improve. It is true that there are certain situations where parents cannot be involved, such as residential treatment facilities, some foster-care situations, and some other programs. That doesn't mean that the "team" shouldn't be involved.

If a child is disrespectful, acting out, depressed, or having other mental health or learning issues, it is far more effective to involve the parent/caregiver in the therapy session. Some therapists are constrained by where they work or who they can see. It is up to the therapist to discuss these issues with their supervisor to always do what is in the best interest of the client.

Our world today is more complex, demanding, fast-paced and confusing than it was years ago. There are many different kinds of families and more new challenges facing parents than ever before, such as multiple divorces, single parenthood, remarriage, stepparenting, same-sex parents, and grandparents raising grandchildren. What matters most is that parent figures are informed, involved, and on board.

Inspiration

Children's Mental Health and Learning Disabilities

Most children are not born with a mental health diagnosis. Often it can be caused by environmental problems, such as trauma, abuse, or violence. Emotional difficulties can also arise when a learning disability is present. The interaction between mental health and learning disabilities is complex and not always clear. Here are five ways in which emotional problems and learning disabilities can interact:

1. Learning disabilities may lead to emotional distress.

2. Learning disabilities may raise or exacerbate existing emotional concerns.

3. Emotional issues may mask a child's learning disability.

4. Emotional issues may exacerbate learning disabilities.

5. Conversely, emotional health may enhance the performance of children with learning disabilities.

What to look for to determine if the child is experiencing emotional difficulties and needs professional help:

- Decline in school performance.

- Poor grades despite strong efforts.

- Constant worry or anxiety.

- Repeated refusal to go to school or to take part in normal activities.

- Hyperactivity or fidgeting.

- Persistent nightmares.

- Continuous or frequent aggression or "acting out."

- Continuous or frequent rebellion and/or temper tantrums.

- Depression, sadness, or irritability.

Mental health conditions, just like physical illnesses (such as asthma and diabetes), are experienced differently by each child. A "diagnosis" does not define the child. Each student needs their own individualized treatment plan, educational program, and accommodation strategy.

It's prudent that teachers and clinicians try not to rush to judgment and assume that all they have to do is set limits with the child/adolescent to rectify the problem. Most parents have already tried every possible trick in the book without any success. They may feel ashamed and hopeless. Instead, offer support and brainstorm together to uncover possible strategies to help the student.

By Mindy Mazur, MPH, educational therapist

Red Flag Behaviors Checklist

Check off the behaviors you are noticing in your child. Follow up with a visit to your pediatrician or a mental health professional. Your observations will aid the health professional in properly assessing the situation.

____ Secrecy (sneaking around, breaking rules, using drugs/alcohol)

____ Frustration (with communication, school, peer and family relationships)

____ Shame (being different, feeling that they are not living up to potential)

____ Depression (clinical and/or situational)

____ Sadness (loss, trauma, loneliness)

____ Boredom (lack of interest and direction, missing opportunities, lacking guidance)

____ Perfectionism (having to be perfect or the best at everything)

____ Lack of clear sense of values or perspective (no structure at home/family, rituals)

____ Isolation (because of appearance, weight, acne, different from peers)

____ Skipping school (fear of failure)

A Mother's Journey

Devon's Story

He was born dead. A tiny, blue baby that could fit in the palm of your hand, just barely four pounds, he struggled for life from the moment he entered this world. The doctors could never really explain why the pregnancy had been so hard or why my son was born seven weeks premature with his lungs collapsed and few signs of life. Or why, after they got him breathing again, he developed an infection in his blood that nearly killed him. Or why he was deaf at birth, and no one figured that out until he was six months old.

No. The doctors could never truly explain anything about my son's health or development. It was up to me, his mother, to figure out what he needed and how to help him, to be his advocate, to keep saying there was another way, to keep trying.

Don't get me wrong, for the most part, the doctors and nurses were great. Doing their jobs as they were trained to do. If it wasn't for them, my son would not be here today, so I am eternally grateful to them all. But there was a gap—a massive gap that lead to intense challenges that, as a parent, I was not prepared for and could never quite find the right resources to help me. I can't even begin to tell you the number of tears I've cried for my son. Back then, if there had been a parenting coach who could have helped me, I would have paid just about anything for their guidance.

Devon was born struggling from day one. After a long stint in the hospital recovering from his birth, he came home. He was the best baby. He never cried, ever. He didn't try to grab things. He didn't fuss. That should have been a clue. But it took us six months and a test from a hearing-impaired nurse, to figure out he that was 100% deaf.

From then on it was test after test, with a few misdiagnoses thrown into the mix. This, combined with his early birth, delayed his growth in many ways. He didn't sit up, roll over, or walk at the age when other kids did. He didn't make sounds. He didn't play.

When Devon was just about two years old, he had surgery on his ears and got 60% of his hearing back. Eventually, that was 100%. I can't tell you the joy I felt when I knew he could finally hear me. The changes in him and his development were instant. And I truly do mean instant. He was so sweet and loving. He could just look at you and you'd know he was happy. He began to smile more and even play.

He went from one day not even able to stand unassisted, to the next day suddenly standing up and running across a room. Thank goodness I had witnesses, or no one would have believed this miracle. He was my miracle child.

But we still had challenges. He didn't talk at all until he was four years old. Anticipating what he was trying to communicate, his older brother would speak for him. It took until he was five to be completely toilet trained. He had a pediatrician, a speech therapist, an occupational therapist, and even a play therapist.

When he went to preschool, he had a full-time personal assistant. But he was always getting into trouble. He had no concept of consequences. Devon could never understand personal space of the other kids. He'd go into their stuff and take what he wanted to play with. He never played with other kids, but loved to play near them. He couldn't make friends. He didn't express any emotion. He didn't like loud noises. He didn't like to be touched. And he couldn't sit still.

So when it was time for him to start grade one, the school and school board called me into what they called a "case conference." This was actually a meeting of government and school officials (including the board child psychologist) where they browbeat the parent into putting their child on drugs. I was overwhelmed, devastated and beat down. There was no one to advocate for me or my son. There was no other choice.

I was a low-income, single mother of two. What did I know?

And so my son was diagnosed with ADHD and put on drugs so that he could go to public school. It was a nightmare for both of us from the beginning. I can't tell you the number of parent-teacher meetings I've had or the number of times the school called because of his supposed behavior issues.

At the start of every school year, we'd meet and create a plan, but it was never followed. Devon continued to struggle, and he fell further and further behind, but they kept pushing him forward, insisting he had to stay with his peer group. And yet he hated them. They bullied him. They made fun of him. He couldn't communicate with them. He got along best with younger children; he wanted to be held back. But the school board refused over and over again.

The drugs changed and got stronger. Soon Devon came up with his own way of dealing with school. He disappeared. He discovered that if he were very quiet and didn't make a fuss, the teachers would ignore him. And they did. He once went three months without writing one word at school. The teacher called me with her concerns only after she discovered that. I won't bore you with what I replied.

Throughout elementary school, it was like sending Devon to prison daily. He was bullied. He failed classes over and over, and my sweet, happy toddler was long gone. He never expressed his feelings. Instead, he would act out in bizarre ways days after an incident. He would pee in the corner or cut the straps off his backpack or take scissors to his dresser, attempting to express his anger and frustration in the only way he could. I could time when to expect an incident. Exactly three days after something happened that would normally frustrate or anger a child, he would act out in some way.

By the time he was 10 years old, he was clinically depressed and suicidal. The doctors recommended more drugs.

I was done with doctors.

I was done with listening to everyone else. I was his mother and while I didn't know everything, I knew my son. We had been on the waiting list for another assessment at the school since grade one. I wasn't waiting anymore.

Against advice, I stopped all drugs. I paid for a full clinical assessment by an independent child psychologist. The diagnosis came back not as ADHD, which everyone had previously insisted on, but as high-functioning autism (a.k.a. Asperger Syndrome, in some circles). He had a very high IQ, extremely low processing speeds, and severe social impairments. Finally, I had something to work with. I did my own research, and we made some changes at home. He joined a friendship circle to learn how to make friends. He went to play therapy to learn how to express his emotions. And he suddenly grew!

He grew six inches in just a few months after stopping the drugs. The incorrect drugs had been stunting his appetite and his growth. He began growing so fast I could barely keep him in clothes! He began to show signs of happiness and we saw some light at the end of the tunnel.

But school was still a big issue. By the time he was in grade seven, I knew we couldn't continue like that anymore. By this time the teachers and kids were bullying him, and he was getting into more and more trouble. He was the problem kid at school and I was the problem parent. I felt like no one was listening. No one would help. And the same issues just kept happening again and again.

We were all frustrated. I knew we could do better. My son was traumatized by school. It was actual torture for him. So once again, I said enough is enough. We were done with public school. I looked at our options and there weren't many. There was no private day school near us and boarding school was not an option. While there were resources for children with severe autism, Devon didn't qualify because he was considered high-functioning. That left homeschooling. I was pretty leery about that.

I'd had my own business for years and worked from home. So homeschooling was a total option; however, could I do it? I went to information events with the local homeschooling association to learn more about it. I researched it online. I talked to other parents. I found a solution I thought we could all live with. It was an online school that provided us with a teacher who specialized in helping kids like Devon.

That first year, we did what is called "unschooling." As a parent, this is REALLY hard to do. It's all about deprogramming and starting fresh. You need to let go of all your ideas of what school should be.

I faced severe criticism and judgments from family members, friends, and even total strangers. On the outside, it looked to others like Devon just stayed at home with me and mostly played video games in his room. But on the inside, he was dealing with the trauma of public school, and healing and rediscovering his curiosity. It was a year of healing for all of us.

I knew it was working when he came to me one day and asked to do some math worksheets. Up until then, I hadn't pushed any official schoolwork. I had totally stepped back and let him learn what interested him. The very words *school* or *learning* would make him cringe. But when he ASKED to learn math, I knew we would be okay.

You see, that is the point. I was meeting him on his terms. I wasn't trying to force him into something he wasn't ready for or a way of learning that didn't work for him. I let him lead. And that made all the difference. He knew what he needed. He couldn't always verbalize it, so by allowing him to take some time and truly giving him a safe space to explore his own learning style, we had a breakthrough.

For most of his life, he had been in fight-or-flight mode. He'd shut down. In his eyes, the only safe place was his bedroom, and the only success he'd had was playing video games. So that's where we started. We talked about all the benefits of video games, from motor control to learning about strategy.

It grew from there. Eventually, he completed official school credits with his online teacher. And guess what? His grades were in the mid-80s. He went from a kid failing every grade to a kid getting excellent grades and thriving. How was this possible?

It was all possible because the school he was now in didn't put him in a box. He could choose how he learned and how he showed his learning. If he didn't show his work in math that was okay, as long as he got the answer correct. He could choose which books to read. He could make a PowerPoint presentation instead of a written essay. It was all up to him but was guided by a qualified teacher who truly cared about him.

We discovered, to everyone's delight, that he was actually a math genius. He was doing it all in his head and just putting down the answer. He was doing algebra in his head! Many times he couldn't describe how he got the answer, so previous teachers had failed him. But now, through conversations with his teacher, she could tell if he knew what he was doing or not.

He developed a very close relationship with his teacher. I know that made all the difference. He had the same teacher from grade eight until graduating high school.

It was all self-paced. He technically went to school 365 days a year because he was always learning. We'd go places and do things and discuss them as a family. He'd come to the grocery store with me and help me figure out the best deals. We were integrating real life with his actual schoolwork. It was amazing.

And then, when he was 15, we had another breakthrough. He wanted to get a job. We knew that a traditional job just wouldn't work, so he decided to start his own business. He began to walk dogs. We created an ad and put it out there, and he had two regular clients within days. The best part, aside from making his own money, was that he met and negotiated with both clients all by himself. For a kid with major social anxiety, this was momentous. He never needed to be reminded to go to work or nagged or any of that. It was 100% self-driven.

There was no turning back. His confidence exploded, and while he still wasn't comfortable in crowds or groups, he could meet and talk to other people one-on-one without shutting down.

He started saving up his money to build his own computer. He taught himself how to build a computer and decided he wanted to go to college to learn computer engineering. For a kid that had previously said he was going to be a bum and live in a cardboard box, and who thought he was stupid, this was another big shift. He now saw that he could do something with his life. He could have dreams and goals.

Up until then, all the teachers in his life had kept pushing him down, telling him not to dream too big. No one believed in him but me and his current teacher.

On the day he sold his Xbox, I think I cried. Video games had been his life for so long. But here he was at 16 years old CHOOSING to do something else. He joined a gym and started working out. I hired him a personal trainer and suddenly Devon was concerned about what he was eating and doing physically. He started going outside more for walks or bike rides. He really started to like how he felt and looked. Together, we bought new clothes for his new muscular physique.

The icing on the cake came when he met a girl in our neighborhood his age, and they started dating. He took her on his first date ever and paid for it with his own money. The excitement and simple pure joy on his face reminded me of when he'd been a toddler, and the kid he used to be before all the mess with doctors and public school.

If I know anything as a mother of a child with special needs, it's that the child will always tell you what they need to thrive in their own way. It may not be a way you understand at first and you may not even agree, but the child knows. By stepping back, loving him no matter what, and letting my son lead, I allowed him to grow into the person he is meant to be, the person he is today.

Now Devon comes to me and we have great conversations. He asks me things like how to be more motivated and what is love and other deep philosophical questions. He is a big thinker. He thinks about stuff all the time. He was never given that chance when he was younger.

I am so proud of the man Devon is becoming. He is kind, loving, hardworking, intelligent, and true to himself. Does he still have challenges? Of course. And he will for the rest of his life.

But I think that by being his advocate, knowing there was a better way, being there for him as he needed me to be, and taking the chance with a different type of schooling despite all the naysayers and critics, as his mother I did all I could to help him succeed. Devon is now truly alive for the first time in his life, and it's only just begun.

By Heather E. Wilson

Stress & Anxiety

Anxiety is a normal part of growing up, and every adolescent goes through anxious phases. A phase is temporary and usually harmless. However, teens who suffer from an anxiety disorder experience persistent fear, nervousness, and shyness, and may start to avoid places and activities. For example, a teen who has an embarrassing moment at school and is refusing to go to school the next day could be reassured and comforted. But that alone may not be enough to help a teen who has been struggling with an anxiety disorder since early childhood overcome this setback.

Some of the things that cause stress in teenagers include academic worries, social media, caring for other family members, friendships, family conflict, body image, work, bullying, discrimination, alcohol and other drug use, tension between cultural worlds, high personal expectations, or high expectations from parents, teachers, and friends.

This section provides techniques to assist teens with managing stress and anxiety at home and in school. Each activity can be practiced in therapy as well as by the teen on their own. Instead of asking teens, "What's wrong?" these exercises allow the teen to uncover and share what they are feeling. Only then is it possible to take the necessary steps to alleviate the issue that is triggering the problems.

Conversation Starters
That Engage Even the Most
Resistant Teens

Open with one of the following to help spark conversation:

- Praise the teen: "I really liked the way . . ."

    Builds self-esteem

- "What was the best part of your day?"

    Shows interest in their lives/encourages verbal expression/connection

- "What's your plan for the day/evening?"

    Encourages strategic and realistic thinking

- "What worked last time you had this problem/issue?"

    Encourages reflective thinking

- "If you could do it again, how would you do it differently?"

    Encourages learning and applying changes

- "If you could do anything really well, what would that be?"

    Encourages reaching for a goal

- "If you could help someone who you know, who would that be and why?"

    Encourages empathy

Sailboats on the Sea: Feeling Focused Art Therapy

Ages: 13-18

Purpose: To unravel and take care of unresolved feelings and emotions. This activity starts out nonverbally and allows for debriefing.

Materials:

- Art materials: Modeling clay or Play-Doh, or markers and paper
- Worksheet: "Debriefing the Sailboat"

Instructions:

1. Give the teen the art materials, instructing them to set them aside until the end of the visualization.

2. Read the visualization script below to the teen while they are sitting on a chair or on the floor.

3. When the visualization is done, have the teen use the clay or paper and markers to create an image of whatever needs their attention.

4. Once this activity is complete, use the worksheet to debrief with the teen.

Script:

Close your eyes and take a deep breath in … now breathe out. Breathe in … and breathe out.

Keep breathing slowly like this. Notice your breath and follow it as it goes in and out of your body.

Now imagine that you are sitting on a peaceful beach in the warm sun, listening to the waves hit the shore. Ask yourself, "Is there something that is in the way of my feeling good?" Put your answer on a paper boat and send it out to sea.

Ask the question again, "Is there something in the way of feeling good?" And put that answer out to sea as well. Continue asking the question and putting the answers on the boats until there is nothing left to get in the way of feeling okay.

When nothing else comes to mind, check in with yourself one more time: "Am I completely okay right now?"

Now ask yourself this question: "How do I feel most of the time?" Maybe it is worried, scared, or mad … and send that answer out to sea as well.

Now put your attention out to sea and look at all your little paper boats bobbing up and down. See all the things that have been getting in your way of feeling okay.

Pick one that needs your attention right now and pluck that boat out of the water.

When you are ready, gently open your eyes and create an image with the clay or draw on paper that thing which needs your attention.

Debriefing the Sailboat

Ask the teen these questions following their art creation:

Once you have taken care of _____, what will that do for you?

_____

What would be the best part about that?

_____

What do you think might get in the way of taking care of this?

_____

What else?

_____

What's the worst part about it? _____

_____

Anything else?

_____

What is one small step that you could take right away to begin to take care of _____

_____

Now make another image with the clay or draw a picture representing the next step you will take.

See, Hear, Feel: 5-4-3-2-1

Ages: 13-18

Purpose: To help manage anxiety, flashbacks, nightmares, sleep disturbances, test anxiety, and more.

Instructions:

Model the following script first aloud and then have the teen practice on their own aloud with you listening. You can restart and repeat until relaxed. If you or the teen becomes sleepy or drifty . . . good, that is really the goal . . . that signals relaxation, and it is okay to stop!

- Name five objects you see in the room, one at a time.

    Example: I see the chair. I see the carpet. I see pens. I see books. I see the door.

- Name five sounds you hear.

    Example: I hear footsteps. I hear the fan. I hear a bird. I hear a car horn. I hear my breathing.

- Name five feelings you are having right now.

    Example: I feel tired. I feel warm. I feel anxious. I feel excited. I feel sad.

- Name 4 objects you see, 4 sounds you hear, and 4 things you feel.
- Name 3 objects you see, 3 sounds you hear, and 3 things you feel.
- Name 2 objects you see, 2 sounds you hear, and 2 things you feel.
- Name 1 object you see, 1 sound you hear, and 1 thing you feel.

Activity

Feel the Feeling: The Only Way Out Is Through

Ages: 13-18

Purpose: To reduce panic, anxiety, and fears.

Instructions:

1. Talk the teen through the following script:

   - *What are you feeling in your body?*

   - *Where are you feeling it?*

   - *Describe what this feels like, looks like.*

   - *What color is the feeling?*

   - *How big or small is it?*

   - *I want you to focus on the feeling and stay with it.*

   - *If you can, close your eyes and keep feeling it.*

   - *Tell me when and if the feeling gets stronger, lessens, or moves to another part of your body.*

   - *Now I want you to take this feeling in your arms and rock it; give it all the love you can.*

   - *Stay with it if you can.*

2. Keep repeating until the feeling significantly lessens or disappears.

3. Then ask the teen if they can try and feel the feeling again (recheck).

4. Show the teen that this is something they can do on their own. By confronting the feeling and staying with it, the feeling is no longer something to be afraid of but something to accept, notice and take care of.

Turning Fear into Courage

Ages: 13-18

Purpose: To confront fears and worries and step into your full life.

Instructions:

Complete the following with the teen.

1. Having the thought, "I couldn't do that, or that's too hard," happens to all of us. But sometimes these thoughts keep us from doing/being all we are meant to. Just for a moment, let's think about the other times when you did something truly amazing and courageous. Write these down here.

   _____

   _____

   _____

   _____

2. If you are having a hard time coming up with your own courageous acts, think of a few people whom you admire for their acts of bravery (big or small). Write their names and acts of courage here.

   _____

   _____

   _____

   _____

3. If you were one of those people, what would you have done in that situation?

   _____

   _____

   _____

   _____

4. For a moment, think of something that you would love to do but can't even imagine yourself doing. Even if you can't do it, close your eyes and imagine the way it would feel to be able to. Describe it here. *(Example: Flying through the air on a trapeze.)*

_____

_____

_____

_____

5. What is something that you have been afraid to say or do because you thought you wouldn't get it right or that you would fail?

_____

_____

_____

_____

6. What or who might stand in the way of doing or saying that thing?

_____

_____

_____

_____

7. Who do you know that would support you in accomplishing this?

_____

_____

_____

_____

8. What are some steps that you could take right now to prepare yourself to do or say that thing?

_____

_____

_____

_____

Talking to Teenagers About Stress

Tips to help support your teen in assessing their stress and managing it with self-awareness.

Stress at the End of the Year

The stress is on. As the end of the academic year nears, pressures for your teenager to boost grades and "finish strong" may increase. Alternately, a feeling of failure and giving up may intensify. Wherever your child falls on this spectrum, we can assume that they are facing some variety of stress as they enter the final phase of this academic year.

On top of academics, your teen may be motivated to get a summer job, which brings its own elements of excitement, competition, and unknowns. They may be dreading the unstructured time of summer, feeling lost or purposeless without school. Or they may be anticipating the freedom and fun of summer so much that it becomes challenging to focus on school. Social life may finally be picking up, causing your teen to worry about whether they will be able to sustain it during summer. And maybe your teen simply feels overwhelmed as they try to balance academics and extracurriculars. These are all potential sources of stress!

The Routine and Stress Connection

Parents often share their observations about their teen's routines with me. As a parent, you are likely intune with what and when your teen eats, how much they typically sleep, how many hours they spend on homework, on their screens, or with their friends. You know which routines serve your teen and which ones are challenging. In other words, you are often aware of your teen's stress.

When you notice a drastic shift in their habits, you, too, may experience stress. For example, if you notice that your teen is no longer spending time with a friend that was previously their "bestie," you wonder what changed. If mornings become harder and your teen is now running late and skipping breakfast, you feel concerned about how they're sleeping and what they are staying up late doing.

Stressed out teens may quickly change habits or routines. When you become aware of this, it can be easy to go into "investigation mode." You want to know what your teen is facing so that you can help them solve it and find relief. These moments require you, as the parent, to slow down, breathe deeply, and focus on connection first.

Here are seven tips for talking to teenagers about stress:

1. **Maintain your own self-care.** If your child is facing intense stress, they will need you to be a sort of respite for them. This doesn't mean you have to be perfect, and it definitely doesn't mean that you are doing wrong by feeling stressed yourself. It simply means

that to show up fully for yourself and your teen, you need to be sure to refill your tank regularly. Reserve time each day to take care of yourself—mentally, physically, emotionally, and spiritually.

2. **Observe behaviors with compassion and curiosity.** The data you have about changes in your teen's routine can help you tap into the stress or worry your teen is facing. As you observe changes, do your best to keep breathing and to act in a calm and collected way. Focus first on connecting with your teen, rather than trying to correct "the problem."

3. **Take your teen's lead.** If you can, and the stress has not escalated to a crisis, use compassion and curiosity as you approach your teen. Wait and see if they will come to you with their challenge first. Once they mention a stress trigger, such as, "I have a massive biology test on Thursday" or "I don't think I'll ever find a summer job," follow up by saying, "Tell me more about that." You may also affirm their feelings by repeating back to them what you heard: "You have a big biology test this week" or "I understand that you don't think you'll find a summer job." Allow your teen to elaborate by gently guiding them to say more using "Is there anything else?" and repetitions until they are finished. This feels more inviting to teens than a series of investigative (yet loving) questions.

4. **Use open-ended questions to tap into feelings.** After your teen has expressed all they need or want to for the moment, you may invite them to explore their stress deeper: "How does all of this make you feel?" A list of feelings can be helpful at this stage. This can also be a good opportunity to ask, "Where are you feeling this (emotion) in your body?"

5. **Use open-ended questions to tap into needs.** Next, you can support your teen in acknowledging their wishes and wants. Ask, "What do you most wish/want to happen?" This is an opportunity for you to listen. Refrain from offering suggestions or ideas. Repeat their wish or want back to them. For example, "You want to start summer with a job that will help you save up for a car."

6. **Use open-ended questions to tap into actions and solutions.** You can invite your teen to practice self-compassion by asking, "What would bring you comfort right now?" or "What would help you feel rested and supported in this situation?" You may also get more specific here as your teen seems ready to problem solve, "What steps have you taken to prepare for the test/summer job/etc.?" and "What else do you feel ready to try?" If you get shoulder shrugs or "I don't know," it's okay to offer a few suggestions or ideas: "How would it feel to take a walk before getting back to studying?"

7. **Take breaks.** Tips 3-6 offer many questions and prompts you can use to support your teen in assessing their stress and managing it with self-awareness. However, they might not have the stamina to answer or reflect on all of these in one sitting. And you might be tired too! Let this be okay. Know that their stress doesn't need to be completely resolved after one conversation. This is a great opportunity to focus on encouragements, such as, "I love you no matter what." Furthermore, rest assured that you have created connection.

In times of stress know that you and your teen are completely normal for having these feelings. At the same time, why not try these practical tips to mitigate stress and improve the quality of life for all in your household?

By Courtney Harris, MEd

Organization & Independence

Attention Deficit Hyperactivity Disorder (ADHD)
Executive Function Disorder (EFD)
Autism Spectrum Disorder (ASD)

The main focus of this section is to create easy-to-understand, simple steps that reduce overwhelm and chaos, thus providing kids with a feeling of accomplishment and independence. Children with ADHD, EFD, and ASD will benefit from the structure provided within these activities.

If the child's skills are delayed or deficient, you will need to intervene with tasks that match their actual developmental level. Sometimes helping these kids is as simple as changing their physical or social environment, altering the tasks you expect them to perform, or changing the way you interact with the child by providing cues, supervision, and encouragement. By building in choices, kids will cooperate more readily as it gives them the control they typically fight for.

Practice difficult tasks in small steps, increasing demands gradually, and using negotiation rather than authority. By developing an environment where you've modified the tasks to match the child's capability, taught them to improve the skills they struggle with, offered support while taking a step back, and used the right incentives to foster cooperation, you will have raised your child to move out into the world armed with a set of skills they can use to tackle problems on their own.

Executive Function Disorder

Purpose: To help you identify executive function issues.

Instructions:

Executive function is the name for a group of essential mental tasks, including planning, strategizing, organizing, setting goals, and paying attention to the important details that will help to achieve those goals. Executive function is what gets us down to business even when we'd rather just hang out.

This checklist will aid you in helping to diagnose executive function issues. If you are noticing multiple issues in the following list, please follow up with your child's teacher and pediatrician.

What do you notice about this child? (Check all that apply.)

___ Difficulty planning

___ Problems organizing

___ Problems strategizing

___ Issues with goal setting

___ Inattentive to details

___ No self-discipline

___ Can't self-regulate

___ No clear sense of time

___ Inability to hold many things in one's mind at once

___ Problems with cooperation and teamwork

___ Not open to new ideas

___ Inability and unwillingness to make corrections

___ Difficulty with memorization and recall

___ Difficulty with questioning and researching

Pom-Poms and You

Ages: 3-9

Purpose: To increase cooperation and attention. Break down overwhelming tasks into bite-size pieces and then reward the child for their effort and completion of the tasks.

Materials:

- 2 jars (at least one clear)
- Colored pom-poms (from craft store)
- Paper cut into strips
- Markers

Instructions:

1. Have the child complete tasks to earn pom-poms to use for a future reward/project. Focus on the problem areas or the areas where the child has not become independent. As the jar fills, say, "Look how many pom-poms you have earned!" Example tasks for earning pom-poms include:

   Before school:

   a. Put on shirt, socks, pants, shoes

   b. Brush teeth/hair

   c. Eat breakfast and clear plate

   d. Ready for school with backpack at the front door

   After school:

   a. Hang up backpack

   b. Complete each homework task

   c. Take bath, put on pajamas, brush teeth, etc.

2. For children ages 3-5, watching the pom-poms accumulate in the jar might be enough of an incentive. After the jar is filled with pom-poms they can be used in an art activity, such as gluing to paper to make a picture.

3. For children ages 6-9, you can give a second reward once the jar is filled. These extra rewards/motivators should not cost money; rather, they should focus on time with the parent, teacher or therapist, doing some activity together.

4. Together with the child, brainstorm a list of activities the child would like to do with you. Here are a few ideas:

- Backward dinner (dessert first)
- Bike ride
- Picnic lunch on the floor while watching a video
- Baking brownies or cookies
- Card/board game
- Manicure and pedicure spa night at home

5. Use the markers to write the rewards on slips of paper and put them in the second jar. Once the pom-poms have filled up the clear jar, the child can pick a "time-together" activity from the second jar.

6. Have more than one child? They can a share a jar and fill it up together, encouraging teamwork and cooperation.

Poker Chips for Electronics

Ages: 5-13

Purpose: To help break down overwhelming tasks, chores, homework, and self-care; and to help reduce parent/child conflict and teach kids that work comes before play. Kids with ADD and EFD can benefit when tasks are broken down into bite-size pieces.

Materials:

- Poker chips (various colors)
- Jar
- Timer

Instructions:

1. Decide the value of each color poker chip (e.g., blue = 5 minutes, red = 10 minutes, white = bonus, you decide). Then decide what tasks will earn which colored poker chips (e.g., brushing teeth = blue chip; picking up room = red chip). Bonus chips can be used when giving extra praise for going above and beyond expectations.

2. Focus on having your child complete a task such as getting ready for school, within a certain amount of time, and mark off completed items on a checklist. For example:

   - Getting dressed: blue (5 minutes)
   - Eating breakfast: blue (5 minutes)
   - Packing backpack: blue (5 minutes)
   - Making lunch: blue (5 minutes)
   - On time at the bus stop: red (10 minutes)

   In this example, this child earned a total of 30 minutes of electronics time that they can use after school BEFORE beginning their homework.

3. A child can turn in their chips in exchange for the time the same day, or they can save all their time for another day. The timer is started at the beginning of the time according to the amount of chips exchanged. Once the chips are used, there is no more electronics time until more chips are earned.

Whistle While You Work:
Taking Care of Belongings

Ages: 3-11

Purpose: To teach children how to break down overwhelming projects into bite-size pieces and promote having fun with chores, and also to reduce parent/child conflict.

Materials:

- 3x5 cards
- Markers

Instructions:

Go to your child's room. Stand right in the middle of it. Look around. How do you feel? If you say exhausted, overwhelmed or frustrated . . . good! That is exactly how your child feels when sent there to clean it up.

1. On each card, write a step that is involved in cleaning up the bedroom. Some examples include:

   - Laundry from floor into hamper
   - Toys back in bins
   - Dishes, glasses to dishwasher
   - Books on shelves
   - Games picked up and stored in boxes
   - Clean clothes hung up/put away

2. When your child comes home from school, tell them that you are going to help them clean up their room. Then hand them one of the cards, and tell them to do what is on the card and then come back to you with the card completed.

3. Put a sticker on the back of the card or draw a happy face to show it was completed.

4. Hand them the next card and so on. Do this every day until your child starts automatically putting things where they belong.

5. If your child cannot read, draw pictures on each card representing the item to be picked up.

6. For teens, use cards or a checklist. Ask them which they would prefer.

7. Keep the cards in a basket in an easily accessible place.

8. Add a timer for more fun!

Give Them a Hook

Tips for helping children with organization:

Teach your kids how to be organized by using the home environment to highlight organizational skills they can carry into school and adulthood. Here are some ideas:

- **Family calendar.** Track everyone's activities on a large calendar that is hung where everyone can see it (e.g., the kitchen). Assign each family member their own color marker for their entries. Always reference the calendar when making plans. Bring the calendar to your weekly family meeting. If you have teens, consider creating a shared Google calendar for online ease.

- **Checklists.** Create lists on 3×5 cards for all activities that have multiple steps, such as bedtime (shower, brush teeth, read story). Encourage your child to create the cards with you.

- **Focus on chores that involve sorting or categorizing.** Grocery shopping, folding laundry (matching socks), emptying the dishwasher and putting dishes away, and other tasks that involve preplanning, making lists, or arranging things are great choices.

- **Always get ready the night before.** Pack lunches, backpacks and lay out clothing to make the morning a breeze and teach your child the importance of planning in advance.

- **Use containers and closet organizers.** Everything has its place. Take photos of toys, clothing, and personal items and tape them to the outside of the container where you want them stored (think kindergarten classroom).

- **Cook together.** Cooking teaches measuring, following directions, sorting ingredients, and managing time—all key elements in organization. Even cleaning up and putting utensils and pans back where they belong makes the task that much easier for the next time.

- **Collecting.** If your child has a particular interest, encourage them to create and organize a collection. Use creativity in this area, and you won't have to spend a penny (just get outside).

- **Be a role model.** Remember that if you are disorganized, your child will follow your lead. Always put things back where they live, keep your living space clear of clutter, and hang up your coat!

FIRST and THEN Board

Ages: 3-9

Purpose: To shepherd children in completing non-preferred tasks in family or group settings. Kids often don't want to do activities that are required of them such as showering, going to bed, homework, etc. Use this activity to move those difficult moments along.

Materials:

- Large poster board
- Glue stick
- Pushpins or tape
- Scissors
- Card stock or a file folder
- Pictures (photographs, pictures from magazines, images from Google images, cereal boxes, household supplies, wrappers, etc.). Every picture should have a label so the child can associate the written text with the picture.

Instructions:

1. A FIRST/THEN Board can be used to communicate a sequence of events or to reinforce completion of a non-preferred activity. This board can be used in a variety of ways:

   - To assist with the transition from one activity to another

   - To assist in completing non-preferred tasks by reinforcing with a preferred activity

   - Breaking a large schedule or sequence of events into smaller steps

2. Making a FIRST/THEN Board:

   a. Gather the materials listed.

   b. Collect pictures to represent activities.

   c. Cut the pictures out and paste them on card stock for durability, or print them on card stock.

   d. Create two columns on the poster. Label "FIRST" at the top of the first column, and "THEN" at the top of the second column.

   e. Attach all FIRST activities under the FIRST column and all THEN activities under the THEN column directly across from the corresponding FIRST activity.

   f. A FIRST/THEN Board can be broken down into two-step activities, for example, "FIRST read a chapter; THEN use the computer."

   g. You can also break down the FIRST into smaller steps, for example, "FIRST put on shirt, pants, socks, and THEN use the computer."

Behavior Charts That Really Work

Ages: 3-9

Purpose: To encourage "start" behaviors (what you want children to do more often). A new twist to the old chart!

Instructions:

Use this worksheet to create a behavior chart for your child that really works!

If you could wave a magic wand over your child's negative behavior, what behaviors would go away because of the impact they have on you and your family?

1. _____

2. _____

3. _____

4. _____

5. _____

6. _____

7. _____

8. _____

9. _____

10. _____

Now, looking over your list, select three behaviors that are creating the most negative impact on you and the rest of the family.

1. _____

2. _____

3. _____

Now prioritize them. Rate these from one to three in importance of getting the biggest bang for your buck:

1. _____

2. _____

3. _____

Let's say that you have chosen "Joey kicking and hitting his little brother" as the top priority. What would you like to see from Joey instead? Be kinder to his brother, play nicely, and keep his hands and feet to himself—right? What we did was to take the negative and turn it around to a positive.

Write down the new, positive behavior here:

_____

Remember to focus on the positive: "I want to see my child playing nicely."
Rather than saying, "I want my child to stop kicking and hitting his brother."

Make a copy of the chart below or create your own. Hang the chart on the refrigerator or in a common family area in the home where the child can see it.

Every time you notice Joey playing nicely with another child, go to the chart and draw a happy face on it. The younger the child, the more frequent the tracking/praise needs to be. The key is to focus on only one behavior at a time. When this behavior improves, you can move on to the second priority, and so forth.

Positive Behavior

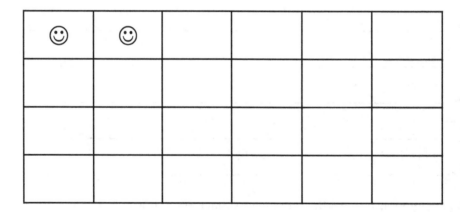

For very young children, getting the happy face will be enough. With an older child, you can tell them that if they earn "X" amount of happy faces they can pick from the reward jar.

The Carrot and the Stick: Why Rewards Sometimes Don't Work

Do you really blame your kids for not wanting to take out the trash, set the table, sweep the floor, or clean up their rooms? Do you want to do it? Does paying them work in the long term? If you've tried the reward system, you know that it doesn't work forever.

Here are some tips to get your kids on board with helping out around the house:

- Explain why doing the chore is necessary. A chore that is not fun or interesting can become more meaningful if you can show your kids that it is part of the bigger picture. Explain that if each family member does one small chore each day you will have more time for the fun things your family gets to do, such as swimming or watching a movie together. Draw a picture of each person's contribution, and show how your family is like a machine with all the moving parts helping the house run smoothly.

- Say out loud: "Yes, I know that this chore is BORING." Let your kids know that you understand that cleaning their room isn't a lot of fun. This isn't a lecture … it is empathy.

- Let the kids do their chores their own way. Don't control them. You can tell them that you want the table set, but you don't have to micromanage where the fork and spoon go. Let them have fun and use their creative minds while doing their chore as long as it gets completed.

- And if all else fails, use the Tom Sawyer method. If you remember the story, Tom is whitewashing the fence and he is not having fun … but then he gets an idea. He tells his friend that painting the fence is not a grim chore, but rather a fantastic privilege. His friend asks to try but Tom won't let him, saying it is way too fun. Finally, he gets his friend to give him an apple to try painting. Soon after, more boys arrive, and vie for the privilege of painting the fence. Pretend you are enjoying washing the dishes—make it look fun—soon your kids will be begging you to help.

Magic Black Bag: How Not to Trip Over Backpacks, Skateboards, Etc.

Ages: 5-16

Purpose: To create organization at home, and to reduce parent/child conflict.

Materials:

- Big, black trash bag

Instructions:

1. Tell your child/teen that by a certain time, 9 p.m. for example, clothes, belongings, etc., must be off the floor and out of your sight.

2. At 8:30 p.m. give the first reminder.

3. At 9 p.m. walk around with a large, black garbage bag and collect everything that was not picked up.

4. Take this bag and hide it in the back of a closet or lock it in the trunk of your car.

5. Tell your kids that they will not get these things back until three days have passed without anything being left on the floor.

6. Stick to it and don't cave. Believe me, by the next night they will be rushing to get their things before you do.

7. The key is consistency, scheduling, and following through.

8. Natural consequences are terrific. If the algebra book ends up in the bag and your teen has to explain to the teacher what happened, most teachers will back you up since they are trying to teach these same skills in the classroom.

How to Outsource Your Laundry for Free: Life Skills Training

Ages: 9-18

Purpose: Most parents struggle with getting kids to pitch in and do chores, and most parents feel like all they do is nag the kids day in and day out. This can lead to explosive behaviors or parents doing everything for their kids to avoid conflict. Either way, a problem is created. Teaching personal responsibility is an essential component of parenting and of raising successful children and young adults.

Parents have described their kid's room in the following ways: "A sea of clothing; wet, moldy towels; science experiments growing—and not the type you get credit for!" "It is so horrifying that I would rather watch the latest Stephen King film than open the door to my son's room." "And to top it off, I have to beg, threaten and coerce to get my kids to hand over their dirty clothing so that I can wash it. Once I give it back, neatly folded, stacked, and clean they don't even put it away!"

Instructions:

1. Purchase two laundry baskets for each child: one white and one another color, and place both inside their rooms.

2. Write out easy-to-understand instructions for your washer and dryer and tape them to the front of your machines.

3. Have a field trip with your kids to the laundry room.

4. Explain to your kids that they will be in charge of their own laundry from now on, including their towels and sheets.

5. Give a laundry lesson and tell your kids that as they undress, the whites go in the white basket and everything else goes into the other basket.

6. Assign your kids one or two days each week that they will "get to" use the machines.

7. Inform them that if they don't transfer their clothing from one machine to the other or remove their clothing from the dryer that they risk having it dumped on the floor by the next person in line to wash clothes.

8. Do not bail your child out. Let them forget; let them find their clothing on the floor, wet and smelly. You are teaching independence, accountability, respect, and consideration for others. You are also teaching that all the household chores should not fall on one person (YOU). You are giving your children a gift for life. And at the same time, you get to stop nagging, you get free time, and it didn't cost you a penny!

Kids as Cooks

Ages: 3-18

Purpose: To teach children life skills for independence, create family time, make chores fun, and streamline the home.

Materials:

- Bread for enough sandwiches to feed the kids lunch for one week
- Cookie sheets or parchment paper
- Luncheon meats, tuna fish, PB & J, or whatever else you and the kids like
- Condiments
- Sandwich bags, foil, or reusable containers

Instructions:

1. On Sunday afternoon, set up an assembly line at the kitchen table: lay out cookie sheets or parchment paper on the kitchen table, along with piles of lunch meats, condiments, peanut butter and jelly, etc.

2. Have the kids lay out all the bread on the cookie sheets or parchment paper.

3. Then have the kids make all the sandwiches using the sandwich options on the table.

4. When finished, have the kids put the sandwiches in sandwich bags and label each one.

5. Put the sandwiches in your freezer where the kids can see the labels. (If you have a deep freeze with a top rack or a bottom freezer this works best for kids to be able to see and reach.)

6. In the fridge or on the counter, have a fruit bowl available where the kids can grab an apple, orange, banana, etc.

7. In the cabinet or on the counter, have a dessert/snack dish available with portion-size snacks available to add to the lunches. (Premeasure the snacks—raisins, cookies, crackers, cheese—into snack-size containers. Kids can also do this and it is cheaper than buying them already snack-sized.)

8. In the morning before sitting down to breakfast, have the kids choose a sandwich from the freezer, a piece of fruit, a snack, dessert, napkin, etc. (If they go to day camp or day care, have them put the items in the lunch box. If you do this in August, getting ready to return to school will be a breeze!)

9. You should also do the same for yourself—think of all the money you will save by not eating out for lunch!

The Creative Brain:
Playing Without Electronics

Ages: 3-11

Purpose: To teach children to play on their own without the use of electronics, and to encourage creativity and brain function.

Materials:

- A paper bag or shoebox
- Stickers
- Markers
- Magazines
- Scissors
- Glue sticks
- Timer
- Index cards
- The "Creative Brain" Worksheet on the next page

Instructions:

Whether you do this as part of a therapy session or as a parent/child activity, work together to create dozens of ideas that encourage hands-on, creative activities that stimulate the mind.

1. Provide children with the materials and ask them to decorate a bag or box.

2. Using the worksheet, brainstorm with the child at least 20 activities they can do alone that are not electronic (no TV, phone, iPad, iPod, etc.).

3. Set the timer for one minute and have the children call out ideas as fast as they can while taking turns. Get silly! Make it fun!

4. Transfer the best ideas onto index cards, either with images of that activity or with the activity name written out. Put the completed index cards into the box or bag, and the next time the child says, "I'm bored, I have nothing to do," or "Can I use the computer or watch TV?" point them to their box or bag and say, "You have so much you can do!"

The Creative Brain

Fun stuff I can do alone:

1. _____
2. _____
3. _____
4. _____
5. _____
6. _____
7. _____
8. _____
9. _____
10. _____
11. _____
12. _____
13. _____
14. _____
15. _____
16. _____
17. _____
18. _____
19. _____
20. _____

Activity

Allowance Is What You Are Allowed: Early Lessons in Financial Responsibility

Ages: 5-14

Purpose: To teach children the consequences of making poor financial decisions and mismanaging their money early on when the consequences are not as severe.

Children are exposed to more and more "stuff" every day, so of course they want more and more. Parents are frazzled because they feel like they are spoiling their children and worry about what that means for their children's futures. Most parents these days have incurred some type of debt like credit card, student loans, mortgage, etc., so they understand what it means to "owe."

Instructions:

1. Each child is allotted 3-5 envelopes (depending on the age, stage, and needs of the child).

2. Each envelope is labeled with something like:

   • *Spending Money* (for little things such as gum, candy, a little toy, etc.)

   • *Lunch Money* (to bring to school)

   • *Bank Deposit Money* (college fund, saving for first car—something BIG and long term. Open a children's savings account and let your child watch the money grow and the interest accumulate. Kids love this!)

   • *Something I Am Saving For* (something your child is asking for that is a bit bigger, such as a new video game, toy, etc.)

   • *Charity* (help your child research and choose a favorite charitable organization)

3. Decide how much you want your child to put in each envelope. For example, if you are giving them $10/week, you might put $1 in spending money, $5 in lunch money, $2 in bank deposit, $1 in savings, and $1 for charity.

4. Pick one day a week (like Sunday morning) to divide up the allowance.

5. Make sure you have dollar bills and change.

6. Hand your child the money and have them divide it up and put it in the correct envelopes.

7. Now for the fun part! Before you go to the store, tell your children if they want to buy anything they need to bring along their "Spending Money" envelope.

8. When you get to the store, do not get involved with the purchase. Let them decide how to spend their money.

9. If they ask to borrow from one envelope so they have more to spend right then, let them, but have them write an IOU to that envelope. Tell them that until the IOU is paid up, each week's "spending money" has to go to the other envelope.

10. Let them feel their successes and their failures. This is a wonderful lesson to give your kids!

Activity

Just One More Glass of Water: Getting Kids to Bed and Sleeping Through the Night

Ages: 3-9

Purpose: To create safety at bedtime and increase the amount of time children stay in their own beds. (Also, to restore parents by getting the sleep they need!)

Do you dread bedtime? Does your child call to you after you have already read three stories, checked for monsters, lined up the stuffed animals, and made sure that the door was ajar in exactly the correct position to your child's specifications? Does your child get out of bed over and over until you are both exhausted and your child is crying?

Does your child demand that you lie down with them? And stay there until they fall asleep? Do you find yourself drifting off and waking up two hours later in your child's bed? Or worse, when you try to sneak out, does your child wake up and demand that you return? Or do you wake up in your own bed and notice the extra little body sleeping peacefully beside you?

If any of this sounds familiar, then you are probably waking up exhausted in the morning, dragging yourself through your day, and dreading the evening when it all starts again. How would you like to be able to tuck your child into bed with a nighttime kiss and have the rest of the night for you? How would you like to wake up feeling rested and refreshed the next morning? Would you like to have enough energy to make it through your day without needing a nap, and actually looking forward to bedtime with your child?

Materials:

- A portable timer
- A special pillow or stuffed toy (you can buy or make this)

Instructions:

1. Remove the TV from your child's bedroom (if there is one).

2. Before dinner, tell your child that there will be a new bedtime plan. Give them the pillow or stuffed animal and tell them that this is their very own Magical Protector. It keeps monsters out of kids' rooms, and helps kids get comfy and fall asleep very fast.

3. Ten minutes before bedtime, tell your child they get to choose two to three stories, but no more. After you read each story, repeat: "Okay, that was story number __. We have __ left."

4.   Tuck your child in. Tell the child that you have a timer and are going to set the timer to go off in five minutes and that you will return to make sure that the Magical Protector is doing its job.

5.   When you go back, reassure your child that they are safe and tell them you will be back again in six minutes. Keep going back with longer intervals in between checks.

6.   If your child gets out of bed, calmly walk them back to bed and repeat from the beginning of these instructions.

7.   If your child ends up in your bed, repeat the drill. I know you are tired, do it anyway!

The average time it takes to retrain your child is about three days (sometimes more and sometimes less). The less you give in, the quicker your success will be and the more rested and peaceful you will feel!

Challenging & Risky Behaviors

Teens, and especially teens with mental health disorders and learning disabilities, are at higher risk for the following:

- **Behaviors that may lead to violence or injury** such as being in a fight, bullying or being bullied, carrying a weapon, self-harm, and considering or attempting suicide.
- **Unsafe sexual behavior:** having intercourse before the age of 13, not using protection during intercourse, and not being tested for HIV or other sexually transmitted diseases. This also includes drinking alcohol or using drugs during or before intercourse.
- **Alcohol, substance, and tobacco use:** drinking alcohol, binge drinking, using prescription or illegal drugs, as well as smoking cigarettes or chewing tobacco, and vaping.
- **Unsafe driving or riding:** driving while texting, driving after drinking or using drugs, not wearing a seatbelt, riding in a car with a driver who has been drinking or using drugs.
- **Poor self-care:** unhealthy eating habits, not sleeping enough, inadequate physical activity, and excessive social media and screen time.

Increased supervision, discussion, guidelines, and communication can lead to healthier kids overall.

Included in this section are tools, activities, contracts, and worksheets to bridge the communication gap and challenges that adults have with teens. Talking about the consequences of choices and actions before disaster strikes often helps in assisting teens to make better choices in the moment.

Inspiration

When Our Teens Don't Get Us and We Don't Get Them ... and What to Do About It

Do you sometimes feel that you and your teenager live on different planets? Do you and your teen get frustrated and angry at each other? Do you notice that your take on a given situation is miles away from your teen's experience? If so, you are not alone. In fact, most parents of teenagers sometimes get mad at themselves for losing control and wonder what they can do about it. Sometimes the solution isn't what you think.

Let me tell you how my son didn't get me and I didn't get him. I want you to know that we didn't just resolve this situation, but I was also able to approach parenting in a whole new way from then on ... and so will you.

Mom's point of view:

A few weeks before my son, Daniel, was leaving for college, I was standing in the checkout line at the Gap with my both of my kids. We had just completed our yearly back-to-school shopping. With every item Dan had selected and had to have, he tossed it to me to carry. Now, I am a petite woman, I was 45 years old, and I had worked all day; it was 9 p.m. We had been in the mall since 6 p.m., and I was exhausted, irritable, weighted down, and broke. In one hand, I was holding two pairs of pants, a sweatshirt, shirt, four pair of boxers, and a sweater. In my other hand was my purse and $250 of clothing that I purchased for my daughter, Sarah, at Old Navy. How did I get here? Why am I carrying all the shopping bags?

There were three checkouts and four to five people in each line. It was a mob scene. I was almost there; I could already feel myself sinking into my bed and nodding off into dreamland. I was dead on my feet. I glanced up at the counter, and two of the checkout girls, not much older than my son, were giggling and discussing what they would be doing when they got off work that evening. I felt as if I had been in this line for 10 days, and I wanted to scream! Instead, I turned to my kids and said, in a whisper, "This is ridiculous!" Dan looked at me with disdain and hissed, "I hate it when people do that ... it's soooooo rude!"

One of the girls looked up from behind the counter and sheepishly said, "I'll be right with you." I was instantly shamed. My more-than-truthful comment made me look like the "mom from hell" to the back-to-school shopping crowd.

Daniel's point of view:

We were at the Gap. Mom was so cool; she was getting me whatever I wanted. I was going off to college and she felt bad. She liked everything I chose. I can't remember a better shopping spree with Mom. She was even carrying everything for me. We got everything I wanted in less than 30 minutes, and there was still plenty of time left to see my friends. It was awesome!

Now it was time to pay. We got in line. The line was really long. My cell phone rang, and it was one of my friends. We talked for a while, and then I told him that I'd pick him up real soon. I had taken my own car to the mall so I could leave as soon as we were done.

My mom was breathing heavily and was looking really irritated and crabby. How can her moods change so quickly? All of a sudden, she blurted out, really loudly, "This is ridiculous!" It was horrible. Everyone in the store was looking at us. I tried to hide and to pretend that she wasn't my mom, so I said, "I hate it when people do that. It is soooooo rude!" Again, all eyes were looking at us, and I looked away, again pretending I didn't know her. Even the girl behind the counter knew how embarrassing it was to be out with your parents. She looked right at my mom and said, with an edge, "I'll be right with you." There, my mom was put in her place.

Now I feel bad: I want to be with my mom, but sometimes she can be such a dork!

— ☆ —

Writing this experience from Daniel's perspective really helped me see where my son was coming from. We had different agendas: He had plans to go out with friends; I had plans to sleep. We had different energy levels: He had slept until noon; I had been up since 6 a.m. I was sad about him leaving for college the following week, and he couldn't wait to get to his dorm and meet his roommate. I showed Dan this piece after I wrote it, and we talked about how we sometimes see things from different angles. After this, I began to take a step back when I was confused about my teen's behavior. I thought about it from his point of view, and then I checked it out with him to see if I was on the right track.

Any parent has the power to do the same thing: take a step back and put yourself in your teen's shoes. You might realize something about your teen—and yourself—that you never have before, and chances are it will improve your relationship.

Inspiration

Raising Teens Fearlessly

What would you do if you were fearless? It's a question asked by coaches, counselors, and gurus around the globe each day, but what does it really mean?

The incredible thing about people is that we are all so completely alike. We feel the same feelings. We experience the same emotions. We have hopes and dreams. We're driven by yearning, and we're driven by fear. Every single one of us.

At the same time, we are each undeniably and startlingly individual. We are unique. And we spend most of our lives struggling to find our place between the two.

Compelled to be accepted, to be loved, and to find community, we embrace our likenesses—we endeavor to assimilate with those around us and to be admitted in. As we conform, the very moment in fact that we fit snugly into the mold, a new longing begins: the longing to be seen. We want to be recognized for that piece of ourselves that is uniquely individual—that secret part of us that is 100% real, that is 100% you.

This is most keenly felt in adolescence, and as the parents of adolescents we have an incredibly challenging job to do. How do we teach our kids to bridge this gap when we're struggling to do it for ourselves?

- We worry about whether we're good parents.
- We worry about the way we're being judged by other parents, teachers, coaches, etc.
- We worry about how our kids are doing.
- We try to give them the tools they need to be successful.
- We try to protect them from harm and from pain and from judgment.
- The list goes on.

I vividly remember one such occasion in my own life as a mom.

Journal entry: April 12th

This morning, my daughter donned a *kigurumi* (a Japanese one-piece hooded pajama made to look like cute animals) and backpack and hopped into the car for the ride to school. It's pajama day at the junior high school.

I know that girls all over town, going for that "this old thing?" glam, are flat-ironing their hair, applying lip gloss, and carefully pairing flannel pj pants with deceptively mismatched t-shirts. My child, on the other hand, has brushed her teeth (I hope) and buttoned up her *kigurumi*.

Cute they may be, but to be clear, she had chosen to leave for junior high school wearing a kind of nappy, slightly dingy, panda suit.

I swallowed hard, and my stomach dropped. It felt like a test. My husband and I have always taught them to stand tall, be themselves, and do what they loved. Who cares what other people think? Who indeed?

BREATHE

"Lilah, I wouldn't be doing my job as a mom," I cautioned, trying not to let any of my own fear seep through, "if I didn't let you know that the *kigurumi* may be a risky choice today."

She shrugged and put on her backpack. Her 14-year-old brother was mortified. "Don't you want anyone to like you?" Max is the reason we drove to school today; a bus ride with the additional social pressure of her in a panda suit felt potentially explosive.

"We have to let Lilah be Lilah," I told him on the drive, copping a line from *Little Miss Sunshine*. But I could see the fear in him: fear for her, for himself, sheer panic for the ridicule that, in his mind, was clearly on its way. I knew where he was coming from. I'd be lying if I didn't admit that I felt it too.

When we arrived at school, Max leapt from the car, shouting not to open her door until he was safely inside. I turned to the back seat in time to see her eyes well up. "Why does he have to be so mean?" she asked.

"People tend to get nasty when they're afraid of something … like being teased," was all I could think of to say. "You know that, Lilah. You know that some kids are going to react meanly … and you've chosen to wear the *kigurumi* anyway because you like it. You can just as easily choose to change into the shorts and t-shirt you packed. You always have a choice."

I fought back the instinct to encourage her to change clothes, the instinct to protect her, the instinct to choose for her. In the instant that it took, she shouted, "I'm doing it! OPEN THE DOOR!" She pulled up her hood and marched into the building without turning back.

My stomach flipped again, but the lump in my throat was all admiration.

— ☆ —

So I ask you, what would you do if you were fearless?

Post Script:

> Lilah got off the bus this afternoon still wearing the *kigaurmi*. When I asked about her day, I got the usual teen banter. Prodding for info about the PJs, she told me that she got a "classic fake 'love your PJs'" from "a notorious mean girl" and her animé friends loved it. She was completely unphased.

The *kigurumi* choice worked out for Lilah that day and Max managed to skirt by unscathed as well. That hasn't always been the case though—they've had their share of sneers, jeers, bumps, and bruises along the way.

And that's OK.

Each time we play all-in, each time we go out into the world as that best version of ourselves, each time we try to stretch ourselves a little farther, we risk rejection. When we encourage our kids to do these things they risk rejection too.

Here's the funny thing about rejection. Sometimes it encourages us, pulls us forward, spurs us on to try harder, to try again. And other times, it shrinks us, pushes us down, and builds up our armor, discouraging future risk. Why?

I've coached hundreds of people. And one thing is true of all of them. Rejection only holds us back when it attaches to our own insecurity. When rejection provides evidence that our deepest fears of not being good enough are the truth, it makes us play smaller the next time. When we see rejection as the other person's problem—then we're inspired to press on.

And this is our challenge as parents: this teaching our kids to play all-in, and to expect triumph, and failure, and all of the "meh" that falls in between—without believing that it's a reflection of who they are.

Here's the bad news:

- You won't get it right all the time—it's just not possible.

- There is no secret decoder ring.

- And the big one … there is no one perfect answer, perfect kid, or perfect parent.

On the flip side of every powerful challenge is an equally powerful solution—and that means there's good news too:

- Mistakes are okay. They're even useful as a way of allowing your kids to see that you're not perfect either.

- You can create the dialogue as you go. You don't need to know what you're going to say. When you're dealing with teens, the more you listen, the more likely you'll be to hear what's really going on.

- And the big one … there are an infinite number of right answers. Don't be so hard on yourself or them.

Life is a series of experiments—not a series of tests that we pass or fail.

By Wendy Perrotti

Difficult Conversations

Sex, drugs, and related issues are all subjects that most parents have difficulty bringing up with their kids. Think back to when you were a child. Who told you about sex? Was it a friend? Was it your mom or dad? If so, how did they handle it and what information did you receive? Was this information accurate? Or did you learn about it on your own as you were experiencing your first relationship? What was your religious upbringing? Were you told that sex was dirty or natural? Were you told to wait until marriage? Or did your mom bring you to the doctor to have you put on birth control? Did your dad hand you condoms and pat you on the back? Our own teenage experiences often have a huge impact on our parenting. We may agree or disagree with our parents on how these subjects were presented or ignored. So before you venture into these difficult conversations with your child or teen, look back at how they were handled in your life.

1. **Get clear about your own morals and values.**

   - How do you feel about teens having sex? Do you have different rules for your own teen?

   - What do you think about kids smoking marijuana?

   - What do you think about underage drinking? When is it okay? When is it not?

2. **Educate yourself about the issues you want to discuss with your kids.**

Get online and find articles about current trends for youth. Make sure that you have the most up-to-date information about the areas that you are focusing on. Remember, not only are you providing parental guidance, but you are also passing along knowledge that your child will need to make thoughtful and appropriate decisions about his or her emotional and physical health.

3. **Make time to talk to your tween/teen.**

Once you know what you want to talk about and have done your research, it is time. If you are nervous or anxious about having this conversation, acknowledge this to your child: "This is really hard and uncomfortable for me to speak with you about, but I am your parent and I need to talk with you about . . . " Be prepared that your child may react negatively to you or say that they "already know all that . . . " Proceed anyway. Give your child printed information or websites to back up what you are saying. If your child argues with you, tell them that you would be glad to hear what they have to say, but first they must research the topic and present it to you just like you did.

Don't wait too long to have these conversations. Kids are experimenting with sex and drugs earlier and earlier. The younger you start, the easier it will be to continue bringing it up. A great conversation starter might be after you and your child have seen a movie with sex or drugs in it. "What did you think about that movie? What did you think about the choices that (fill in character name) made? What would you have done? Do you have any questions about anything that you saw?"

If your child ignores you or doesn't want to talk about it, don't give up! Keep looking for opportunities to bring up those uncomfortable issues. Soon you will notice that it isn't so awkward after all!

What are your own feelings about:

How do you feel about teens having sex?

_____

_____

Do you have different rules for your own teen?

_____

_____

What do you think about kids smoking marijuana?

_____

_____

What do you think about underage drinking? When is it okay? When is it not?

_____

_____

What are the drugs of choice in your community?

_____

_____

How much supervision do teens really need?

_____

_____

Out with Friends Unsupervised

I know that going out with my friends without parental supervision is a privilege. I know that you love me and want to keep me safe. You respect that I am no longer a small child and want the privilege of going out with my friends without your supervision. Therefore, we both agree:

1. I will always tell you where I am going to be, who I am going to be with, and what I will be doing.

2. If I am going to be at a friend's house, I will share the address and phone number with you.

3. My curfew is _____(time). This can be negotiated between us. My curfew means that I am inside my home by this time.

4. I understand that I must let you know as soon as I come home.

5. I will always call and ask your permission if my plans have changed and will not go anywhere without checking in with you first.

6. I understand that you have the right and responsibility to check up on me not only when you feel the need, but from time to time just to keep me safe.

7. I will respect the limits and guidelines of my friends' parents.

8. I agree that if I am unable to keep up with my responsibilities, such as my schoolwork and chores, I can lose the privilege of going out with my friends.

9. I understand that I can call you at any time if I feel threatened or unsafe when I am out with my friends. I will not be punished for getting myself out of a bad situation.

10. The consequences for not following through with these guidelines for going out with friends unsupervised are:

    a. _____

    b. _____

    c. _____

Teen Signature: _____ Date: _____

Parent Signature: _____ Date: _____

Inspiration

Good Role Models for Teen Drivers

Before you drive anywhere in your car this morning, think about some of the messages you are sending to your kids and start acting like you want your kids to act.

- Wear your seatbelt.
- Don't exhibit road rage.
- Don't use your cell phone.
- Avoid distraction.
- Don't tailgate.
- Don't drink and drive EVER.
- Be courteous to other drivers.
- Take care of your car inside and out.

Write up a contract with your teen that explicitly states the rules and responsibilities of driving. A sample contract is provided on the next page to help you get started.

Issues to address in your contract are:

- Consequences for drinking/using drugs while driving
- Speeding and cell phone use
- Curfew with the car
- Who pays for what (gas, insurance, maintenance, etc.)
- Driving and use of the car being a privilege and not a rite of passage into adulthood

Parents and teens will sign the contract and then post it in a prominent area of the house so there are no arguments, no exceptions. Break the rules, lose the privilege.

Teen Driving

I know that being able to drive the family car is a privilege. I know that you love me and want to keep me safe. You respect that I am growing up and that I want the privilege of using the family car. Therefore, we agree:

1. I will follow the rules of the road, staying within speed limits.

2. I only have permission to use the car at these times: _____.

3. I must be home with the car by: _____.

4. I agree to not use my cell phone or other electronic device while driving.

5. I agree not to leave the gas tank empty and to contribute my share to gas. My share is: _____.

6. I agree to pay my share of the car insurance. My share is: _____.

7. I agree to follow the law and your rules about having other people in the car. These laws and rules are as follows: _____.

8. I agree to always wear my seatbelt.

9. I agree to call you if I am unable to drive the car for any reason.

10. I will not use alcohol, marijuana, or any other drug while operating the car and will not transport anyone who is using drugs or alcohol as they can be a huge distraction to the driver. Instead, I will call my parents and discuss the situation.

11. The consequences for not following through with these limits are:

    a. _____

    b. _____

    c. _____

Teen Signature: _____ Date: _____

Parent Signature: _____ Date: _____

Inspiration

What You Need to Know About Your Teen and Drugs and Alcohol

Do you suspect that your teen is using or abusing alcohol or drugs? Is there a nagging feeling in the back of your mind that tells you that you really need to check this out? Are you afraid of what you might find? Do you worry when your son or daughter is out with friends for hours on end and you don't know where they really are?

Then join the ranks of parents raising teens today all over the world. In almost every interaction I have with parents of teenagers, the topic of drugs and alcohol comes up. Parents don't know what to do: "Should I search his room? Should I confront her? Should I demand a drug test? Will I drive an even bigger wedge into our already distant relationship? Maybe it's just normal that she is experimenting ... but her moods have changed. I am frightened for my teen's safety."

Here are some possible warning signs of teen alcohol or drug use:

- Missing school or work

- Not saying where they are going

- Lying or being vague about where they have been

- No longer interested in activities that they used to enjoy, and not replacing them with other fun activities

- Borrowing money from parents or friends and unable to explain loss of money or valuables

- Sniffling, runny nose, dilated pupils, or red eyes

- Loss of appetite or eating too much

- Associating with a new group of friends, maybe those who use drugs

- Hiding things that would show alcohol or drug use: liquor bottles, rolling papers, or pipes

- Moodiness, change in personality, avoiding you

What you can do?

- Supervise your teen: Know where your teen is and what they are doing.

- Plan: Decide what you will say before you talk to your teen if you suspect alcohol or drug use. (Avoid negativity and express your concerns with care and love.)

- State the facts: State what you know from the above warning signs.

- Be open: Listen to what your teen has to say.

- Set and enforce rules and guidelines: With care and concern, let your teen know that you will not put up with drug or alcohol use/abuse. "I know you can't stand it when I make rules, but I am your parent and it is my job to keep you safe." Hold your teen accountable for his or her actions and set clear consequences for not obeying your rules. (Offer outside help such as therapy or rehab for severe situations.)

- Be prepared for obstacles: Many teens will become very angry and defensive and walk away from you. Take a deep breath and go back for round two.

- Keep talking: Any chance you get, make an attempt to talk with your teen. Don't give up or lose your temper, no matter how uncomfortable the situation might seem.

- Design a contract: The contract should outline the rules and their consequences. Both you and your teen need to sign it. Be clear, firm, and concise.

- Follow through: Be consistent. The minute you back off or avoid your teen, they will run with the freedom.

- Know this: Your teen wants you to rein him or her in. It is scary having so much power and no one noticing that you are getting away with breaking rules. Being out of control is not that much fun for your teen either.

Parent Ammo: The Written Word

Getting through to a teen who is in denial can be impossible. One method that has good results is research and the printed word. The following parent did research and then confronted her teen with the physical complaints that he was using not to go to school. The teen was denying using marijuana. June was able to direct her son toward information that was on the internet (which he believed).

"Dear Susan,

Here is an excerpt from an article on the effects of long-term marijuana use. It really took away Joey's excuses, especially after all the medical tests showed he was in otherwise good health.

I highlighted below the symptoms that Joey has and deleted some parts of the article which were long winded so that Joey would at least look at it. He smiled and I think he said I "booked him," which means he's not getting away with it anymore.

Keeping fingers crossed, June"

Symptoms of Marijuana Use:

- Sleepiness
- Difficulty keeping track of time
- Reduced ability to perform tasks requiring concentration and coordination, such as driving a car
- Increased heart rate
- Potential cardiac dangers for those with preexisting heart disease
- Bloodshot eyes
- Dry mouth and throat
- Decreased social inhibitions
- Paranoia, hallucinations
- Impaired or reduced short-term memory
- Impaired or reduced comprehension
- Altered motivation and cognition, making the acquisition of new information difficult
- Psychological dependence
- Impairments in learning, memory, perception, and judgment
- Difficulty speaking, listening effectively, thinking, retaining knowledge, problem solving, and forming concepts
- Intense anxiety or panic attacks

Write Me an Essay

Ages: 13-18

Purpose: To educate teens about the consequences of their choices and create meaningful, healthy conversations between parents and teens.

Instructions:

1. Have your teen write you an essay according to the situation. Some topic ideas include:

   • Marijuana's effect on a teenager's brain

   • How STDs are contracted and what happens to your body

   • What is date rape and what you can do to be safe

   • Drinking and driving, and why it is dangerous

   • Texting and driving, and why it is dangerous

   • Available jobs and pay for people who don't finish high school

   • Prescription drugs and addictions

2. Guidelines for the teen:

   • Length: 250–500 words, double-spaced, spell-checked

   • Must be at least a "B" paper

   • No privileges until paper is turned in to the parent and discussed together

Our Own Teenage Years

Whether you're a parent, therapist, or teacher, it's always a good idea to check in with our own experiences and triggers. Use the questions below to stay in check with yourself.

1. When you were a child/teen, what do you remember about anger in your home?

    _____

    _____

    _____

    _____

2. How did your parent(s) handle anger/emotion?

    _____

    _____

    _____

    _____

3. How did you feel about how anger was handled?

    _____

    _____

    _____

    _____

4. How do you handle anger and frustration now?

    _____

    _____

    _____

    _____

Responsibility & Independence

Most teens would love the opportunity to dream, plan, and imagine their future. These fun, thoughtful and engaging activities can be used with teens individually as well as in groups to open up new perspectives and opportunities beyond the present moment.

Some key things to keep in mind:

Get out of their way and encourage them to begin to solve simple problems on their own so that they strengthen their confidence muscle to solve more complex problems on their own. Let go of perfectionism. Really. PERFECT isn't available to any of us, so in other words, give them space and refrain from criticism. Failure is okay and even beneficial. Through failure and mistakes come the learning.

Continue to reevaluate as you increase the teen's responsibility, independence, and freedom. Is your teen ready to drive to school by themselves, cook for the family once a week, or babysit a younger sibling? What decisions can they begin making on their own? If you've given too much freedom and a negative situation arises, it's important to talk about it, increase the supervision, and try again in smaller steps.

Getting this right is the key to raising successful, healthy, and happy teens.

What Ancient Greece Can Teach Us About Teens

"The children now love luxury; they have bad manners, contempt for authority; they show disrespect for elders and love chatter in place of exercise. Children are now tyrants, not the servants of their households. They no longer rise when elders enter the room. They contradict their parents, chatter before company, gobble up dainties at the table, cross their legs, and tyrannize their teachers."

Sound familiar? While this could be said of our modern-day society, this quote is attributed to Socrates, who lived nearly 2,500 years ago.

With the explosion of technology, today we experience the world in a very different way than people did back then. Before us at any moment are a host of diverse images, sounds, videos, ideas … you name it, we are constantly bombarded by stimuli. We have the ability to know what is going on in every corner of the earth and beyond. At the press of a button we are able to talk to people all over the planet. The amount of information we consume has grown exponentially and continues to do so every day. Perhaps a blessing, perhaps a curse, it depends on how you look at it.

But I would propose that even in our 21st century world, teens share more similarities than differences with teens millennia ago—not to mention with teens who grew up before the year 2000.

What teens have today that they didn't in the time of Socrates:

- social media
- smartphones
- cars
- skateboards
- movies, video games
- 24-hour stores

What teens have today that they *also* did in Socrates' time:

- puberty
- the opposite sex
- drugs
- desire for independence, privacy, and a happy household
- disagreements with their parents
- peer pressure

- friends
- confidence issues and uncertainty
- the need for love and security
- anger and rebellion
- not always making good choices
- caring about what their friends/peers think of them
- the need for positive role models

So teens are teens are teens! While the outside world changes, the inner world repeats itself again and again.

As a parent, remembering your teen years and sharing your own experiences is one of the most important steps you can take in having a close and open relationship with your child.

Spend some time reflecting on some of the thoughts you had when you were their age. How about some of the mistakes you made and consequently learned from. What would you do differently than your parents did in how they related to you? What would you do the same?

— ☆ —

Ancient Greece also has something to teach us about the relationship of a mentor in a child's life.

Back then, children were not educated in order to get a job, but to be good citizens of their country. Nowadays, a case can be made for the opposite being true. In general, our children are pushed through school systems, not in hope of them being a good person, but so that when they have graduated, they can get a job and support themselves and their future families.

Keeping this in mind, a large load of the responsibility of raising a good citizen has fallen on the shoulders of the parents, no matter how busy they already are with their other responsibilities and commitments. Most parents don't have anyone else to share the burden with.

A crucial part of a privileged teenager's education in Ancient Greece was a mentorship with an elder. The teenager learned by watching the elder discuss politics, by helping perform his public duties, and by exercising with him in the gym.

Today's mentor-mentee relationships may look a little different, but the purpose is the same: spending time with somebody who has "gone through it all," and is now able to reflect on that time and be a guide.

Back then, this right was reserved only for the rich, but today many more resources and opportunities are available to teens of every social standing. Thousands of books have been written, clubs and groups are available, social programs are in place, and mentors and coaches are specializing in exactly this service.

By Daniel Rosenkrantz

The Wonders of Positive Communication

How your teen behaves does not need to affect the relationship you have with them.

"Did he just write what I think he did? How can this be so? My son tells me he hates me. My daughter rolls her eyes when I ask her to do something. Of course this affects our relationship!"

Your teen's behavior has the ability to affect your relationship because of three things:

You feel violated. In other words, you take what they are doing personally. "He wouldn't say he hated me unless I gave him a reason to hate me."

You feel frustrated. "Why won't my teen just do what I tell him to do? Why does he have to make a big deal out of everything!?"

You feel disappointed. "I wanted my teen to be well behaved and respectful. He's a menace to society!"

If you don't take what your teen does personally, if you investigate and practice strategies and parenting techniques that work, and if you don't give up hope, you will be able to see past bad behaviors. You will be able to see him once again as that lovable being that you brought into the world.

It's easy to think that the way things are right now is the way that they will always be. But this is far from the truth. Your child becomes a teen and before you know it he is moving out of the house.

Work on having a great relationship with your teen, no matter how bad they seem to act.

By Daniel Rosenkrantz

Great Relationship

Purpose: To look at our normal, or habitual behavior, identify it, and figure out what we would like to replace it with.

Instructions:

1. Make three columns and label them respectively: Emotional Trigger, Usual Response and Preferred Behavior.

2. First identify an emotional trigger, something that provokes an emotional response in you. One example may be when your daughter says something disrespectful to you. Write this in the first column.

3. Next, write in the second column your usual response to this. Becoming aware of our automatic responses is the first step to changing them.

4. In the third column, try to identify how you would rather respond.

Example:

Emotional Trigger	Usual Response	Preferred Behavior
I ask Mary where she is going with her friends, and she tells me to mind my own business.	I scream, "You're not going anywhere unless I know where it is!"	I calmly say, "Please don't talk to me that way. I love you and feel responsible for keeping you safe."

This exercise can also be done by your teenager. Come together and discuss both of your findings. These can be effective data points in fostering a discussion of how to improve communication between the two of you.

Here are a few tips for fostering positive communication:

1. **Ask open-ended questions.** This may sound simple, but so many of the questions we ask are for efficiency rather than further conversation.

    Here is a closed question:

    > **You:** How was school?
    > **Teen:** Good.

    And here is an open-ended question:

    > **You:** What did you discuss in history class today?

> **Teen:** Well, we were talking about …
>
> **You:** Oh, that's really interesting. What do you think about … ?

2. **Find out what your teen is excited to talk about, and talk about these things more.** If it is music, then talk about music. If it is science, then do some reading and strike up an interesting conversation about microbiology and outer space!

3. **Answer the questions that your teen asks you.** If you expect a response from them when you ask, be open with them when they return the favor. If they ask, then most likely they are interested in your response.

Have a real conversation: ask a thoughtful question, listen to the answer, and respond appropriately. And be ready to answer some questions yourself!

By Daniel Rosenkrantz

Teenager's Budget Plan

When I was 15 years old, I got my first summer job making salads at a local pizza place. I would go in at around 4:00, work until 10:00, and then happily take a pizza to share with a friend. It was a great summer and I saved around $2000. Unfortunately, it wasn't too long before that sum dwindled to nearly nothing. Here are some ways that (unlike me at 15) your teen can make money, spend money, and *still* have some savings.

Perhaps you are familiar with the structure of a common child's allowance plan, in which a certain amount is given to the child by the parent and then divided up into different envelopes: Savings, Something I am Saving For, Charity, and Spending Money. The parent decides with their children how much goes into each envelope weekly.

With the teen savings model, the numbers will be a bit larger (with weekly paychecks or other small job sources), but the principle is the same.

If your teen doesn't already have a bank account, help them open one. Once you know the rough amount that they will be making each week at their job, sit down with them and design a budget that you both can agree upon. Here is an example:

Steve is making $150/week mowing lawns in the neighborhood:

Savings: $80 (directly into the bank)

Something I Am Saving For: $15 (e.g., the amusement park trip coming up in a few weeks)

Spending Money: $40 (e.g., going to the movies, gas money, etc.)

Charity: $15 (which is roughly 10% in this example) or whatever amount seems appropriate. This would also be a good opportunity for your teen to research different charities and pick a favorite one that he likes.

Each budget line should make sense. Saving without reason doesn't always register for teens—or adults, for that matter!

The money that goes directly into the bank every week should remain untouched until at least their 18th birthday. This can be thought of as a self-made trust fund.

Having a summer job can be a great way to learn responsibility, budget funds, and have a fun and rewarding summer all in one!

By Daniel Rosenkrantz

Inspiration

What Teens Want

Even though times have changed since you were a teenager, teens still want and need the same things as you did when you were their age. These are my personal reflections on being a teenager at the turn of the 21st century.

Part I: What Teens Want: Independence, Privacy, Belonging, and Love

Independence

During the teenage years, parents want to keep an even greater eye on their teen because they believe that it is in these years that they are most at risk. Your teen wants the exact opposite. Denial of this longing for independence results in a clash of wills.

Too much oversight can actually have the opposite effect than what was intended. Lack of independence causes anger and far greater rebellion from your teen than perhaps would occur if certain small liberties were granted.

For example, one Halloween my mother didn't want me to go trick-or-treating. But I wanted to—my friends and I had been looking forward to this night for a long time! She said "no" but I went anyway, walking out of the house in a huff, while she stood at the door watching.

My friends congratulated me on taking matters into my own hands. It was only later that night, when my father found me and brought me home, that I learned how upset my mom was and the reason for her not wanting me to go out.

The communication between us just before I went out had been something like this:

    Mom: I don't want you to go out tonight.

    Me: Why not?

    Mom: Because I don't.

    Me: What do you mean? I'm going!

    Mom: No, you're not.

    Me: My friends are waiting for me! I'm going!

This is the best way for your teen to do the exact opposite of what you wish. With little or no explanation, you can almost guarantee your teen will do what they deem to be the appropriate action.

Seeing your teen as a young, independent adult who wants to make their own decisions is a step in the right direction and may help to open dialogue around developing and respecting the house rules.

Before saying flat-out "No," find out what freedoms your teenager wants and have a discussion about why they may or may not be awarded these. Tell them how you expect them to behave and tell them very clearly what will happen if they break the rules.

Negotiate the rules together with your teen and don't be afraid to compromise. Rules made together will have a longer-lasting effect as well as a greater chance of being abided by.

Have these kinds of discussions far in advance of the time when the rules will come into play. If your teenager is expecting to go out on Halloween and has made plans for many weeks ahead, telling them "no" just before they are walking out is not going to go over very well.

Privacy

Do you notice that your teen keeps his door closed a lot more than he used to? Do you hear him pause the phone conversation when you pass by his room?

This is not necessarily because he is saying or doing things that you would disapprove of, but merely because he wants his own life, with parts that others don't know about. Just as we all have our private lives, teens want the exact same thing.

Privacy, though, should not be confused with not telling you things that as a responsible parent you need to know, like where your teen is going to be until they come home.

Let your teen know that you want them to have their privacy, but in order for you to feel comfortable with this, a few things have to be agreed upon. These agreements can be reached by making trades with your teen: "You can have your own phone, but you have to tell me where you are going when you go out. If you are out and go somewhere else, text me and let me know where you will be. If you keep me posted about what's going on in your life, I won't need to ask."

Trust is a necessary prerequisite to privacy.

Belonging

If your teen doesn't feel love, a sense of belonging, or comfort at home, they naturally look for it elsewhere—most likely from their peers.

Until now, their family has been their main support system. But now your teen finds support from their friends instead, on issues that their family doesn't necessarily talk about (e.g., sex), or that they feel you have no idea about. Their friends (what I will call their "second family") are people whom your teen feels safe and welcome with, or at least feels a sense of belonging around.

This second family is not guaranteed forever, as the home family seems to be. If one of the members ceases to fit in, they may not be part of the family in the future. This, of course, creates certain pressures, expectations, and codes in the "second family" structure.

What we call "peer pressure" now becomes a subtle but influential mode of operating. Peer pressure can be merely what your teen sees her friends doing, and wanting to be accepted by them, therefore does the same things.

Even when your teen feels uncomfortable by what this new family is doing or how they are acting, they won't leave because it is better to have an imperfect family than to have no family at all. They may very well take part in these things that they don't agree with because they want to stay a part of the family. This is when poor judgment and high-risk behaviors may occur.

Love

Teens want to feel appreciated, respected, and loved, just like every human does.

As a parent, it is important to create a safe and loving home environment. Even when your teen inevitably learns a lesson—sometimes the hard way—you can always provide them with a place to come back to where they will not be judged by the choices they have made, but instead they will be supported through this process of change and growth.

Part II: Your Role as Parent

So what can you do as a parent to make these transition years, these years full of new choices, a positive experience, both for your teen and for yourself?

Share your own experiences. Being open and honest about your past—telling your teen about similar experiences that you had—will create a bridge between the two of you that you can both walk on. If your teen knows that you once stood in their shoes, they will be much more likely to come to you with questions about the things they are currently facing.

Peace negotiations. As a relationship of trust and understanding is formed, make it clear to your teen that even if they do something that they fear they will be punished for, they will not get in trouble if they come to you and talk to you about it. Grant them amnesty for what they are willing to discuss with you. Use this valuable opportunity to have a real dialogue.

You are not giving your teen permission to act as they wish, tell you about it, and then go do it again. Instead, you are giving them permission to make a mistake or a choice and then learn from it. The more dialogue that you and your teen have and the more trust that there is between the two of you, the less likely they are to go out and make the same decisions again.

Govern by example. Demonstrate and model in your own life what you feel to be the right way of action and decision making. Even if your teen would not necessarily make the same decisions as you, they will see that you are living in accordance with what you believe, that your values are what your decisions are based on.

Stay current. Anything that your teenager wants to know, they will find out. Know this and stay at least even with them, if not one step ahead. Especially today, when every little bit of information is just a click away, it is important that parents know what their kids know.

Be a reliable source. Create a space where you become the first reference point for your teen's curiosity. By being open and honest as a regular practice, you, the parent, will push Google to second place and will become a trusted source and example for your teen to reach out and touch.

Find positive role models. I am not talking about someone on TV. When your teen has someone in their life who they really trust and look up to, it can make all the difference. Your teen needs people who they can emulate and strive to be like. Surround your teen with people who are making good decisions in their lives and people who have had similar experiences to what your teen is having. Every teen can use one, or many, positive role models in their life.

Part III: Taking Action

Luther Burbank, renowned American horticulturist, botanist, and humanist, wrote the following in his book *The Training of the Human Plant*:

"Above all [when raising children], bear in mind repetition, repetition, the use of an influence over and over again. Keeping everlastingly at it, this is what fixes traits in plants—the constant repetition of an influence until at last it is irrevocably fixed and will not change. You cannot afford to get discouraged. You are dealing with something far more precious than any plant—the priceless soul of a child."

As parents, consistency in behavior and action is essential to successfully raising a teen. Repetition is the secret ingredient that allows your best intentions to work wonders in your home.

So are you ready to have a closer relationship with your teen, one based on mutual respect, openness, and responsibility? Be consistent and know that you have the power to meet and overcome all challenges that come your way.

By Daniel Rosenkrantz

Coach a Teen: Getting Started

Ages: 13-18

Purpose: Therapists and teen coaches can use this to structure the session and create a sense of safety and control for the teen.

Instructions:

Ask the teen to take a few minutes at the start of your session to answer the following questions. If they have a hard time coming up with anything, provide some examples.

- What were your successes since we last saw each other?

- What were your challenges?

- What would you like help with or to talk about today?

- Would you like to brainstorm some ideas?

- What was the best part of your week?

- What was the worst part of your week?

- What's happened since we last spoke?

- If your best friend was telling me about your week, what would they say?

- Here's a piece of paper and some markers, would you like to draw a picture of your biggest challenge?

Teen Coaching Check-In

Ages: 13+

Purpose: To check in with the teen and guide discussion during the session.

Instructions:

At the beginning of your session together, check in with the teen using the following questions.

What were your successes since we last saw each other?

1. _____
2. _____
3. _____
4. _____
5. _____

What were your challenges?

1. _____
2. _____
3. _____
4. _____
5. _____

What would you like help with or to talk about today?

1. _____
2. _____
3. _____
4. _____
5. _____

Visions of Hope:
"If You Could Wave a Magic Wand"

Ages: 15+

Purpose: To help teens get in touch with their dreams and desires.

Instructions:

Take the teen through this series of questions:

- If you could wave a magic wand, where would you like your _____ (grades, motivation, relationship, goals, life, etc.) to be at within the next _____ (six months, one year, five years)?

- If it turned out just like that, what would that give you?

- What would be the best part about it?

- Why?

- Back to the present, what do you think could be slowing you down or getting in the way of having what you just described?

- Anything else?

- The way things are right now, how is this affecting your _____ (grades, motivation, relationship, choices, life, etc.)?

- What's the worst part about this?

- Why?

- Pulling out that wand again, what if you could get where you want to be and it was fun and easy?

Let's create a plan to get you there. What are three small things that you would like to do this week to move you toward your goal?

1. _____

2. _____

3. _____

Teen's Wheel of Life: Assessment and Tracking

Ages: 13-18

Purpose: To engage teens in talking about the different facets of their lives. It can be used week to week to set goals and monitor growth.

Materials:

- "Teen's Wheel of Life" template
- Markers or colored pencils

Instructions:

- Using the following "Teen's Wheel of Life" template, tell the teen to rate on a scale of 0 to 10 (0 being "Not at All Satisfied or Happy With" and 10 being "Completely Satisfied or Happy With") the section of their life that you are discussing (e.g., school, friends, etc.). Or, if you want a full assessment, you can have them rate all of the sections on the wheel.

- Ask them to draw a line on each triangle and number it based on how they rated this area. Then have them shade this section in using colored pencils or markers. For example, if they rated "friends" as a 2 out of 10, then they would shade in 20% of that triangle. (If you are doing a full assessment, have them repeat this for each section of the circle.) When done, date the wheel.

- Once they have completed a given area (or the entire wheel), you are ready to debrief their design with them.

- Use this exercise from time to time to demonstrate progress or to pick a new area to work on.

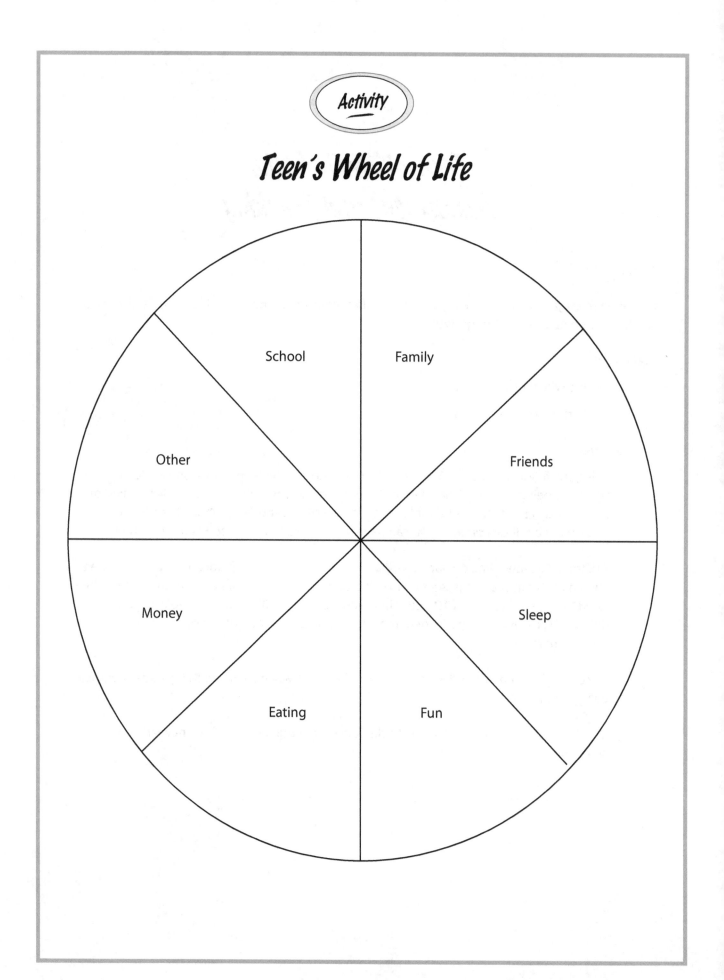

Teen's Wheel of Life

Activity

School

Family

Other

Friends

Money

Sleep

Eating

Fun

Debriefing the Wheel

Ages: 13-18

Purpose: To deepen the "Teen's Wheel of Life" experience and get to the core of the issues; to create a plan of action and accountability.

Instructions:

Using the teen's completed Wheel of Life, go through these questions with them:

Pick an area to tell me about.

- If _____ was a color, what color would it be?
- If _____ was a fabric, what would it feel like?
- If _____ was an 8 or a 9, what would it look like?
- What is one thing you can do this week to move up a point?

Additional questions to spark discussion:

- What do you make of it?
- How does this look to you?
- How do you feel about it?
- Can you say more?
- How does that fit in with your plans?
- What do you think that means?
- What do you want?

Dear Best Friend

Ages: 13+

Purpose: To instill motivation, hope, and a sense of control over their future through a visioning exercise for teens.

Materials

- Paper
- Pen or pencil

Instructions:

1. Give the teen a piece of paper and a pen or pencil. Let them know that they will be writing a letter to their best friend.

2. Read this before they begin:

   It's about a year from now. You are looking back over the past year knowing that you have worked through a lot. You are no longer feeling _____ and _____; in fact, you are very satisfied with your current life. You sit down to write a letter to your best friend, describing the year. The letter starts with:

   Dear _____ (friend's name),

3. Next, here are some prompts to ask and answer in the letter to their best friend.

   - What were your successes in the past year?
   - What were your challenges in the past year?
   - What did you have to do to overcome those obstacles?
   - What did you discover/learn about yourself during this period?

4. If needed, help construct the letter.

Copyright © 2019 Susan Epstein. *Creative Interventions for Challenging Children & Adolescents*. All rights reserved.

Dear Best Friend (Responsible One)

Ages: 13+

Purpose: To encourage teens to be responsible by giving advice to others. This activity can be used in group therapy sessions.

By encouraging teens to give advice to their peers, they can often benefit by listening to someone else's problem. Also, by distancing oneself from a problem, it is less threatening and easier to offer solutions.

Instructions:

1. Instruct each member of the group to write a brief letter to someone he or she really trusts. The letter should consist of a request for advice concerning a real problem—present or past. In their letters, members should include enough facts and feelings so that the other group members will be able to relate.

2. The letter should be signed with a fictitious name.

3. Collect the letters, and then pass them out again, ensuring that everyone will receive a letter that is not his or her letter.

4. Instruct the group members to write a response to the letter they have.

5. When the group finishes, have the group members read the letters and their responses aloud. Allow the group members to discuss the advice given, debating whether they agree or disagree, and why. The therapist can also guide the process to reflect appropriate advice if need be.

Dream Boards

Ages: 13+

Purpose: Visualizing goals and setting intentions to complete these goals, creates a higher likelihood of success. Use this nonverbal activity with teens individually or within a group or family meeting (if in a group setting, have the teens share their boards and state their dreams aloud).

Materials:

- Poster board
- Glue stick
- Scissors
- Magazines
- Camera
- Printed photo of teen

Instructions:

Getting Started

1. Instruct teens to start flipping through magazines looking for pictures, images, or words that they are drawn to or that light them up.

2. Guide them a bit until they get the idea: What do you want to do in the next six months? What do you want to accomplish? What sport or activity do you want to try? (Keep the questions coming!)

3. Cut out the pictures and set them aside.

Creating the Dream Board

1. Take a photo of the teen, print it out, and give it to them to paste in the center of the poster board.

2. Take the pictures from the magazines and paste them to the board all around the photo.

Action Steps

1. Tell the teen to place this dream board where they will see it every day.

2. Tell the teen to look at the board first thing in the morning and before bed.

3. Check in with them from time to time and ask them if anything that they have put on their dream board has happened!

A Perfect Day!

Ages: 13+

Purpose: To mine for goals and dreams in teens.

Instructions:

Have the teen spend a few minutes thinking about what a perfect day would be like in his or her life. Encourage writing a story describing in detail everything about that day. The following prompts will help them get started:

Where are you?

_____

_____

_____

Who are you with?

_____

_____

_____

What are you doing?

_____

_____

_____

How do you feel?

_____

_____

_____

Social & Emotional Skills

Social skills activities for boosting teamwork, self-control, and emotional savvy are important. Negative and antisocial behaviors put teens at risk for losing friends, depression, losing control, angry outbursts, violent behaviors, harming self or others, school failure, and lifelong emotional and social problems.

Kids who develop social skills will be better equipped to deal with their peers, difficult situations, and life problems. They learn prosocial skills through watching and listening to others, as well as though teachable moments, experience with social rules, and firm, fair, and consistent discipline.

Parents and therapists will find these worksheets and activities useful in creating plans with kids who have previously made poor choices and engaged in antisocial behaviors such as stealing, bullying, vandalism, etc. Note that volunteering is the number one activity that can make a huge impact in turning a teen's behavior around. Helping others with no expectation of monetary reward can be the shift that can propel teens onto the path of success.

Parent Activity

Volunteering: Getting to Thank You!

Purpose: To give without getting something material or tangible in return, and to teach empathy, the benefits of helping others, and how to make a difference. Teens who have issues are often called out on their negative behaviors; here is a chance to allow them to feel appreciated and valued. Volunteering usually comes with recognition and a thank you which can contribute to a teen's self-esteem.

Instructions:

1. Remember a time in your life when you volunteered or performed an act of service for another person or organization.

2. Looking back, how did it feel?

3. Now imagine that instead of volunteering you had been paid to do that work. How would that have changed the experience for you?

4. What did you take away from your experience?

5. If you are a therapist, how can you include volunteering or being of service to others in your treatment of children and families?

6. If you are a parent/caregiver, what opportunities are there for your family to do something together for another person or organization?

7. Work with the teen to create a quick list of possible volunteering activities for them. Say, "Let's brainstorm. I'll go first." Get silly, everything goes. Write down any ideas you think up. See how many you can list in 10 minutes—set a timer!

What Is Your Word?

Ages: 13+

Purpose: To encourage children and adolescents to find something meaningful to put at the center of their lives in order to overcome suffering and depression.

Materials:

- Paper
- Art supplies, such as paint, colored pencils, markers, etc.

Instructions:

Keeping positive messages front and center gives us something to focus on to create success in our lives.

1. Ask the teen, "What is the one word that best describes you?" Answers could include *artist*, *peacekeeper*, *leader*, *comedian*, *computer whiz*, and so on.

2. Help the teen come up with a word that best describes a positive attribute that he or she has.

3. Give the teen a piece of paper and have them draw, color, paint, and/or decorate that word so it is big and bold.

4. Make five copies of this paper and send them home with the teen to hang in the bedroom, kitchen, bathroom, and so on, so that they see this message multiple times a day.

5. Use the "Positive Attributes List" on the next page to stimulate the conversation.

Positive Attributes List

Use this list to dig deeper and find more words that describe your teen in a positive light.

adventurous	compassionate	enthusiastic
brave	conscientious	faithful
bright	considerate	friendly
calm	courteous	funny
careful	creative	generous
communicative	determined	gentle
loving	diligent	hardworking
loyal	easygoing	helpful
modest	patient	honest
neat	polite	kind
optimistic	reliable	thoughtful
sociable	sensible	warmhearted
sympathetic	sincere	

Tweet Power

Ages: 13+

Purpose: To encourage teenagers to express themselves.

Instructions:

Some teens aren't very conversational. This challenge will get them talking to you.

1. Tell the teen, "On Twitter you only get 280 characters to express yourself. I will ask a question, and you respond by writing an answer using 280 characters."

2. Allow them to use the computer with a word processing application to count the characters.

3. Use the "Tweet Power" worksheet on the next page for examples of questions.

Tweet Power

Tell me something you accomplished in the last week.

_____

_____

Tell me about something you did that you were proud of.

_____

_____

If you could do anything in your life, what would it be?

_____

_____

If you could go anywhere, where would you go?

_____

_____

Are you an introvert or an extravert? Explain.

_____

_____

What do you think that real friendship means?

_____

_____

What do you think your life purpose is?

_____

_____

Creating Greatness

Ages: 13+

Purpose: To encourage teens to strive for greatness and success by examining others and themselves. This activity can be used in individual or group therapy sessions.

It's typical for teens to see themselves as "less than" or just "average." These labels can turn into feelings of self-loathing and at times lead to depression and other mental health issues.

Everyone has something they are great or exceptional at. Finding it and pointing it out to teens can help them uncover other interests they can develop to increase self-worth and build confidence.

Exploring definitions of the words *average* and *exceptional,* and exploring behaviors that are connected with these labels, can be eye opening for everyone—even parents!

Instructions:

Use the worksheet, "Creating Greatness," to engage the teenager during the session. After the teen has filled out the worksheet, use this as a conversation starter.

Creating Greatness

1. Write down the names of people you know who are average achievers. (Average: usual or typical, mediocre or inferior.)

2. Write down three times in your life when your average achievements actually caused you to come up short.

3. Write down the names of people you know who are above average or exceptional. Explain how they are different from "just average."

4. What's one small thing you can do going forward to be great or exceptional?

Excuses Versus Reasons

Ages: 13+

Purpose: To help teens take responsibility for their actions and to help them move forward toward success.

Teens are quick to make excuses when they are ashamed or embarrassed. Often teens will lie due to fear of punishment, ridicule, and being seen as "less than." Encouraging them to take responsibility allows them to grow and learn from their mistakes. Offering alternative reasons for their actions encourages them to see the bigger picture.

Instructions:

Use this with the teen during the session. This will help to begin a conversation and create a teachable moment.

Share the following with the teen:

Excuses are never the reason why one does or doesn't do something. They are merely a revision of the facts construed to help one feel better about what did or did not happen. For example:

Excuse: You didn't turn your homework in because the dog ate it.

Reasons are the logical facts associated with a behavior. It forces personal responsibility where it is appropriate. For example:

Reason: You didn't turn your homework in because you left it where the dog could get it.

Have the teen answer the following questions:

1. What are some of your favorite excuses?

2. What are the real reasons behind your excuses?

3. How do you feel when you use an excuse?

4. How does using an excuse keep you from being the best you that you can be?

Time, Time, Time

How do you spend your time each day? Answer the questions below. Then, to better see how your time is spent, use the following two worksheets to track your current week and to create a goal week.

1. How much time are you at school each day?

   _____

2. How much time do you spend on homework?

   _____

3. How much time do you spend at meals?

   _____

4. How much time do you spend sleeping?

   _____

5. How much time do you spend doing some type of sport or activity?

   _____

6. How much time do you spend doing homework and seeking help for that homework?

   _____

7. How much time do you spend with friends doing something fun?

   _____

8. How much time do you spend on the internet, playing video games, social media, texting, and so on?

   _____

9. How much time do you spend watching TV?

   _____

10. Of the activities you do, which ones do you think are time wasters?

   _____

   _____

What Does Your Week Look Like?

Sunday	Monday	Tuesday	Wednesday	Thursday	Friday	Saturday

What Would You <u>Like</u> Your Week To Look Like?

Sunday	Monday	Tuesday	Wednesday	Thursday	Friday	Saturday

Engagement, Cooperation & Learning

Attention Deficit Hyperactivity Disorder (ADHD)
Executive Function Disorder (EFD)
Autism Spectrum Disorder (ASD)

Developing successful students requires their engagement and cooperation. Making schoolwork meaningful and fostering a sense of competence is essential. Welcoming students' opinions and ideas into the flow of the activity and using informational and cooperative language with the students will have positive effects on their engagement. Giving students the time they need to understand and absorb an activity by themselves will provide a sense of autonomy for the student, thus increasing confidence and mastery.

Students with ADHD, EFD, ASD, etc., often struggle with school and homework. Having structure and flexibility around homework assignments, and having them know why they are being asked to do a particular assignment, helps immensely to promote cooperation and learning. Both parents and teachers will find these activities to be useful and applicable not only to children with learning challenges but to all students in a variety of learning situations.

Engaging Students in School

Instructions:

The list below includes key components in students being actively engaged in learning, conversation, and discovery.

Use this checklist when looking at why students might be disengaged, bored, or disruptive in class or at home with homework. Answer yes or no to each.

The activity . . .

• Activates prior knowledge.	**Yes / No**
• Fosters active investigation.	**Yes / No**
• Promotes group interaction.	**Yes / No**
• Encourages collaboration.	**Yes / No**
• Allows for choice.	**Yes / No**
• Includes games and humor.	**Yes / No**
• Supports mastery.	**Yes / No**
• Nurtures independent thinking.	**Yes / No**
• Does not make children wait.	**Yes / No**

Three-Stage Plan for an Amazing School Year

Purpose: To assist parents and professionals in creating a new treatment plan.

Instructions:

Beginnings are a great time to look back and evaluate your expectations, goals, and aspirations. We learn from our mistakes, we learn from certain decisions and choices that seemed right at the time, and we learn, too, that even with the best intentions sometimes those choices led us down a rocky road.

Have the parent/caregiver answer the following questions to help engagement in a treatment plan:

1. What was the best thing that happened last school year?

2. What was the worst thing that happened?

3. If you could do something over again, how would you handle it?

4. What advice would you give yourself for this new school year?

5. What do you know now that you wish you knew a year ago?

6. What are your concerns for your child today?

7. What is your dream, goal, and vision for this school year for your child?

Take **one thing** you want to improve or change, and break it down into three steps:

1. _____

2. _____

3. _____

My Special Project

Purpose: To promote learning, excitement, and engagement in children and adolescents outside the school environment, and to increase self-esteem, confidence, creativity, motivation, and presentation skills. This activity can also be used in a group therapy format.

Materials:

- White board, paper and pen, or computer

Instructions:

Providing a creative learning environment at home is an exciting way to stimulate a child or teen's mind. Try this activity at home.

1. Schedule a family meeting and tell the kids that everyone in the family is going to have a chance to create and showcase his or her own project. It can be whatever they want.

2. Brainstorm ideas such as designing a garden, creating a workspace in the basement, looking for rocks, or creating a presentation about something else of interest. The ideas should be something they want to do.

3. Next, ask them what supplies they will need for their project and create a list.

4. Gather the items together or shop for them if you don't have them.

5. Pick a day—could be a Saturday, Sunday, or a vacation day—and mark it as PROJECT DAY on the calendar.

6. Tell the kids they have from 8 a.m. until 4 p.m. (or whatever time frame works) to design, create, and finish their project.

7. After dinner (this night would be a fun night to get a pizza), have each family member stand up and show off his or her project.

My Own Report Card Goals

Ages: 9+

Purpose: To give students useful and purposeful feedback on their school experience without associating it with a grade. For kids with attention deficit hyperactivity disorder (ADHD), mental health issues, and/or learning disabilities, report cards can be demoralizing and hurtful. Oftentimes, grades do not reflect the effort that a student puts into his or her work.

Instructions:

At the beginning of the quarter or semester, ask kids for their top five learning goals. At the end of the quarter or semester, use the worksheet on the following page to help the child/teen create their own report card that reflects effort, not grades.

My Top Five Learning Goals: (What I want to learn this year)

1. _____

   _____

2. _____

   _____

3. _____

   _____

4. _____

   _____

5. _____

   _____

My Own Report Card

1. How did I do?

   _____

   _____

2. Did I succeed in learning what I set out to learn?

   _____

   _____

3. Do my grades reflect my effort?

   _____

   _____

4. What were my obstacles? Challenges?

   _____

   _____

5. What did I excel at?

   _____

   _____

6. What needed more attention?

   _____

   _____

7. What subject or topic did I love learning?

   _____

   _____

8. What bored me to tears?

   _____

   _____

9. What type of learning do I like the best: Watching? Listening? Doing?

   _____

   _____

The ME Poster

Purpose: To increase motivation, self-esteem, and sense of purpose for children and adolescents; this activity can be used in individual, group, family, home, and classroom settings.

Instructions:

Work with the child or adolescent to create a poster about themselves that shows them doing something they are proud of or that offers encouraging words.

Go to the Big Huge Labs website to create your own motivational poster: bighugelabs.com/motivator.php

Activity

"Getting Unstuck" Cards

Ages: 13+

Purpose: To help teens move on from being overwhelmed, from suffering from writer's block, or from obsessive thoughts. This activity can be used in individual, group, home, and classroom therapy settings.

Materials:

- 3×5 cards
- Colored markers

Instructions: Brainstorm statements, questions, or prompts that create excitement for the teen. Have the teen create a stack of at least 10 cards to use when he or she is stuck. You can create your own cards using 3x5 index cards.

The following are examples of prompts:

- What would my best friend do?
- What am I resisting?
- What is needed?
- What are other possibilities?
- Where do I limit myself?
- If I were at my best, what would I do now?
- What does it mean to be focused?

We All Have Homework

Ages: 5-13

Purpose: To engage children in being independent in completing homework, and to create a fun learning environment.

Instructions:

Insist that homework is your child's responsibility and not yours. You don't need to sit down next to your child when they are doing their homework, but you do need to be available (this means that you could be making dinner or you could be sitting with your laptop across from them doing your own work).

1. Tell your child: "I am going to work while you work. We all have 'homework.'"

2. If your child says, "Mommy, I can't do it, I need your help," then go and sit next to your child and read the directions again aloud. Take one step at a time, have him do the problem and explain it to you out loud. Watch your child do the next problem by himself to make sure that he understood.

3. If he gets stuck, go through the steps again and show your child how he can do it on his own. This way he will not be relying on you for every detail.

Be a Helper, Not a Doer

Purpose: To encourage children to work on assignments while providing company, reassurance, and clarification, or directions.

Sometimes when we want to help our kids succeed we get carried away and end up doing their work for them. It is important to be clear with your children that you've already been to school and now it's their turn. When a child does something on their own with some help from you, they can feel really proud that they accomplished it. When you do it for them, they may not do well at school because they have not integrated or understood the assignment themselves.

Instructions:

Brainstorm some ways that you can be a helper, not a doer, and list them below. Examples might include breaking down assignments into manageable steps, talking through problem areas without solving problems, or encouraging kids even when it's difficult.

Ways I can be a helper:

1. _____

   _____

2. _____

   _____

3. _____

   _____

4. _____

   _____

5. _____

   _____

When's the Best Time to Do Homework?

Agree on specific times for doing homework ahead of time and then stick to it. In our home, our kids came right home from school, got a snack, and then we pulled the homework stations up to the kitchen table. (I had a rolling cart with everything that they needed.) After that we would have dinner. As the kids got older, they had to go back to their studies after dinner.

After-school programs:

Now, you may have kids who play sports and have to stay after school, so this may be a little more challenging for you. It is important that their homework gets done and they get to bed on time. Post the hours that homework will get done and stick to it (barring illness or other things when life happens to you).

Make an agreement with your child:

Write down your agreement: "We do homework between the hours of 4 and 6 p.m. in our house." Fill out the homework agreement on the next page and hang it on the homework station or on the refrigerator. When your child says to you, "Mommy, can so and so come over?" You can say, "Well, we are not going to do that because our agreement is that homework gets done between 4 and 6." "Well Mom, I finished my homework and it's 4:30; now can my friend come over?" "Absolutely, you've done the homework first, now you can have a friend over or you can go out to play."

Remember:

- You are a helper, not a doer.
- Praise their efforts, not the end product or how smart they are.
- Insist that homework is your child's responsibility, not yours.
- Chunk the homework into bite-size pieces using a timer.
- Consider getting a tutor, if necessary.
- Agree on specific times for doing homework and post that agreement in a place where all can see it.

Parent-Child Homework Agreement

Homework will begin at _____ (time) and end at or before _____ (time).

If homework is completed before _____ (time) _____ (name) will be able to do the following activities:

1. _____

2. _____

3. _____

4. _____

5. _____

Child/teen signature: _____ Date:_____

Parent/caregiver signature: _____ Date:_____

Setting Up a Homework Station

Ages: 5-13

Purpose: To provide a designated space for storing supplies and completing homework. What this will teach your child is self-discipline, organization and planning. And in return, this will give you less stress and more free time (remember, taking care of you is taking care of your kids).

Materials:

- A specific area in your home (not their bedroom) where your child will not be distracted by TV or other things.

- A credenza-type desk or a trifold poster board to help block off distractions.

- A white board or chalkboard: Set up the board where they can log in their homework and check off what they have done. This also helps when planning out long assignments. When your child comes home from school, have them write their assignments on the white board.

- School supplies: Pens, pencils, scissors, glue, tape, rulers, etc.

- Pockets or boxes for supplies.

Key points for parents:

- Get your child involved; take them shopping for supplies.

- Buy supplies in advance; have extras and things you may need for school projects.

- If you have more than one child, make sure they each have their own homework station.

- Make sure your child is not slouching and not doing homework on the couch.

- Inspect homework every day for completeness (if need be).

189

Organize and Chunk Out Homework

Ages: 5-13

Purpose: To help children manage homework without getting overwhelmed. This activity is especially helpful for children who struggle with ADHD.

Grouping assignments into similar chunks is very helpful for kids who have difficulty sticking with tasks and not getting distracted and for kids with shorter attention spans, such as children with ADHD.

Materials:

- Timer

Instructions:

1. Say to your child: "We are going to do 10 minutes of math. Then we are going to take a break, and then we will do 10 minutes of reading. After that we'll take a break, and then we will go back and finish the math."

2. *Important:* Make sure to take the breaks after the agreed upon homework time has elapsed. Set the timer during periods of homework and also in between assignments. During the breaks from homework play a game with your child (something quick like I Spy, Uno, or tic-tac-toe).

3. *Remember:* Keep them involved, chunk the time according to your child's age and their developmental stage and any issues they might be having with attention.

"I Hate Homework!"

Purpose: To increase a student's engagement in homework and to eliminate power struggles, tantrums, and meltdowns.

Instructions:

Parents and teachers can encourage school engagement by creating and supporting assignments that have a purpose. Ask these questions before assigning homework or while looking over a homework assignment. Getting a "yes" to these questions will increase the student's willingness to complete the assignment and will increase engagement in learning:

Does the student have a choice as to how the assignment is done?

_____

_____

Does the student have a choice where the assignment is done?

_____

_____

Does the student have a choice on how much time it will take to complete the assignment?

_____

_____

Does the assignment engage the student in something new, or is it a regurgitation of something already taught in class?

_____

_____

Does the student understand the purpose of the assignment?

_____

_____

Does the assignment augment learning already begun in class?

_____

_____

It's the Effort That Counts

It is important to praise your child's efforts and not just the end product. Talk to your children about the path and the work that leads to goals being achieved.

As your child is sitting there doing problem after problem, praise them on what a good job they are doing with sitting still, putting the pencil to paper, and getting that homework done. Even when the going gets tough and they get frustrated, say:

> "I am really glad that you've been keeping at that one."

> "How about we leave that problem, the one that's giving you a really hard time. We will come back to it later today. I know how hard you are working at it."

By praising the child's efforts, it encourages them to do their homework the next time.

Alternatively, if you tell them how smart they are, what are they going to do the next time to be smarter? Your child may feel like they have to live up to those expectations, which could lead to more stress and anxiety. Those kinds of compliments are passing—they feel good for you to say, but do not help your child develop their own self-worth.

Parent Worksheet

Homework: LDs, ADHD and Other Challenges

You may be asking yourself: "After trying the methods already given in this book, why am I still having problems getting my child to complete his homework?"

Answer these questions about your child:

- Does my child have difficulty learning?

- Has my child been suspended from school?

- Has my child's teacher written on the report card that he is not working up to his potential? Or that my child appears "lazy"?

- Does my child have stomachaches or headaches a lot?

- Does my child not want to go to school?

- Does my child feel demoralized?

- Is my child already taking medication?

Kids diagnosed with ADHD or another disability usually have learning disabilities as well. These learning disabilities include executive function disorder, auditory and visual processing disorder, dyslexia, dyscalculia, dysgraphia, dyspraxia, integration sequencing, and chronic distraction.

More fundamental changes may be needed to attain the results you are after. Ask yourself: Could lack of any of the following be contributing to the problem?

- Structure

- System

- Sleep

- Nutrition

- Respect

If so, then you may need to implement a workable system and a solid structure by creating new habits and routines such as:

- Regular bedtime

- Regular mealtimes

- Not having a TV in the bedroom and fewer electronics around in general

- Healthy diet: providing high protein/low sugar foods and as many fresh, whole foods as possible

- Knowing your child's whereabouts

- Being around (or having somebody be around) when your child is getting their homework completed

- Being consistent in your communication by letting them know that they cannot disrespect you. Use your words to convey your message:

    "Please don't speak to me that way."

    "That's disrespectful."

    This is how you model for your children how you want them to talk to you.

You can do it!

Implement a strong back-to-school program and instead of your child saying, "No, I won't do my homework and you can't make me," you'll have less battles over homework and more fun times together.

Inspiration

Tutors and Mentors

For additional homework help, you may consider getting a tutor or a mentor. Extra help with homework can be just what you need if you're always battling with your child and don't want to be the bad guy anymore.

Where do you find a tutor? A tutor could be:

- An older child in your neighborhood

- A high school student

- A middle school student if your child is younger

- An older cousin or even an older sibling

- Someone other than you!

If you are having issues with a high school student or they are struggling in school, having a tutor can really take the edge off and help your teen feel successful. Having someone their own age or close to their age is also a way of role modeling for teens. If an older student tutors a younger student, your son or daughter may want to be a tutor to someone younger in return!

Children From Different Cultures

As classrooms, clubs, and communities become more multicultural, hidden challenges arise. Understanding what is going on for these children helps professionals working with children and parents come to constructive solutions that will develop acceptance of diverse cultures as well as give all children the opportunity to develop to their full potential as adults.

The seven key emotional needs of children are:

1. To be accepted (to belong)
2. To be loved
3. To feel safe
4. To feel supported
5. To be trusted
6. To be understood
7. To be valued

When children's emotional needs are not met their behavior often goes off track. Children from different cultures face additional challenges in their lives in having these needs met.

Here are some challenges to consider:

- Language barriers can leave a child feeling isolated and not understood.

- Being teased, mocked, or bullied by other children for being different can make a child feel unsafe, unloved, unsupported, and not a part of their environment.

- Discrimination by adults in authority can build chronic resentment toward authority.

- Parental stress from coping with their new environment may mean a disconnected environment at home which affect a child's behavior and learning outside the home.

- Traumatic past experiences, especially for those who have migrated from war-torn countries, can affect a child's ability to settle in class, concentrate in learning, and get enough sleep at night.

The solution for these children requires a holistic approach that includes support for the family. Often children pick up the language and new culture they live in quicker than their parents, which leaves parents struggling to manage. Parents who are unfamiliar with their new environment need to be guided on what is available to them to support them with the challenges they face.

These children require understanding and compassion when their behavior is indicating that their emotional needs are not being met and they are not feeling that they are okay. Rather than see them as "difficult" children, see them in need.

Here are some suggestions for teachers with children from a different cultural background than themselves:

- Educate yourself with accurate information about the culture of the child to minimize misunderstanding. Some things that are acceptable in one culture are not in another, and a child being punished for something that is considered okay in their culture is confusing.

- Take a moment outside of lesson time to connect with the child.

   Are they able to express what is going on for them or is language a barrier?

   How are things at home?

- Build a good rapport so that you become a trusted adult in their life when things become difficult for them.

- Observe the child's interactions with other children in the classroom and at recess.

- Make an effort to connect with the family. Parents may be shy to approach you because of language and cultural barriers. If parents are not engaged, pursue why this is the case; perhaps they did not understand the instructions on school notices and don't understand what is expected in your school culture. The way they were schooled may have been very different from the way their children are being schooled.

- If a child starts to display behavior that is angry, attention seeking or even withdrawn, then begin with connecting and listening before trying any correcting.

- Most importantly, reflect on your own thoughts and beliefs about the culture the child is from. Any judgmental thinking on your part will influence the relationship with the child and limit your success at connecting with the child. Children have a very keen ability to pick up prejudices, even when we try to hide them.

- Another key reflection as a teacher is to check your expectations of the child. If you expect less from a child from a different culture, you will get less from them.

Here are some suggestions for parents with different religions and customs and from a different cultural background than the place in which they are currently living.

- Build a strong relationship with your children and ensure that the challenges you are having do not overwhelm you to the point that you are unable to be there for them when they need you. Your children may struggle to find how they fit into their new environment. It may appear they are rebelling or challenging your beliefs, customs, and values now that they are in a new environment. The reality is that they are trying to figure out how they fit in.

- Ask for help!

- Believe your children. When children come home and tell you that they are being treated differently than other children, believe them. Children face subtle mistreatment that is hard for them to articulate and hard as a parent to fight against.

These are some examples:

— More disciplinary consequences than other children.

— Less attention and assistance in learning.

— Condescending and patronizing language or tone of voice.

— Less acknowledgement for effort and results.

One of the most important factors in mitigating these hard-to-deal-with situations is to build a relationship with your children's school and their teachers. Children whose parents are actively engaging with their teachers are less likely to experience discrimination.

By Kathryn Jones

Connection, Communication & Positivity

Attention Deficit Hyperactivity Disorder (ADHD)
Oppositional Defiant Disorder (ODD)
Autism Spectrum Disorder (ASD)

It may seem obvious, but the best way to connect with your child or teen is to actually connect with them. In our busy world, parents and kids alike are spending more time on electronic devices than with each other.

Kids who suffer from mental health disorders need our attention even more now. Focusing on a few areas will certainly make a big difference in the connection you have with your kids: family meals, spending a few moments at bedtime to check in and say goodnight, sharing ordinary time and moments like inviting your child to come grocery shopping with you, creating a special time together, showing affection, staying involved with their school, friends, activities, and above all, staying interested in their lives.

This section contains tips, worksheets, and activities designed to strengthen the bond between parents and kids. These tips will enable parents to create a warm home where children are listened to, parents are mentors, and the family is a loving unit. Also addressed are special challenges such as blended families and how to navigate, "You're not my dad!" type situations. The family mission statement is key to mapping the family vision, rules, and boundaries.

Inspiration

Puddle Parenting:
Seizing Opportunities of Joy and Connection

Several years ago, I pulled up to the dry cleaners to drop off a few winter coats. It was a damp day; the rain had stopped, but the aftermath of the storm had left the parking lot full of puddles. I sat in the car for a few minutes before getting out, watching a dad with his two-year-old boy navigate the lot with a big basket of laundry on their way to the laundromat next to the dry cleaners.

Dad carried the laundry, and the two-year-old had a small bag, too. At the edge of the sidewalk was a puddle. His dad's back was to him, and the little boy walked right through it. He turned around, and a glorious smile appeared on his face.

He turned around to check where his dad was—his dad was still walking—and then the little boy jumped back in the puddle and stamped his feet. His smile got bigger; the child's joy was classic. Next he got up onto the sidewalk—by now, his dad was struggling with the door to the laundromat—and the little boy went back to the puddle for yet another jump.

At this moment, his dad saw him. A look of anger and frustration now crossed his dad's face, and he grabbed the little boy's arm and dragged him into the laundromat.

This made me sad. I thought of all the missed opportunities that busy, stressed-out parents, caregivers, and professionals give up for the "have-to-dos."

The next time you see a puddle, I challenge you to get in there with the child or teen in your life. It doesn't have to be a literal puddle, but the opportunity to stop, watch, and join the absolute joy that splashing together can provide.

Strengthening the Parent/Child Bond

Instructions:

Use this worksheet to help parents who have a negative or distant relationship with their child. By modeling positive interactions and collaborative strategies, parents will feel closer to their child, and the child will be more cooperative.

1. I love you: Tell your child daily that you love them—no matter their age. Even on trying days or after a parent-child disagreement, when you don't exactly "like" your child at that moment, it is more important than ever to express your love. A simple "I love you" goes a long way toward developing and then strengthening a relationship.

   These are the times of day I will tell my child I love them (e.g., before they leave for school, when they come home, and before bed):

   _____

   _____

   _____

2. Teach your values and beliefs: Tell your child what you believe and why. Allow time for your child to ask questions, and answer them honestly. Reinforce these teachings often.

   The following are my basic values and beliefs:

   _____

   _____

   _____

3. Create a special name or code word: Create a special name for your child or a secret code word with your child that is positive and special that you can use with one another. Use this name as a simple reinforcement of your love. The code word can be established to have special meaning between you and your child that only you two understand.

   Our secret code word is: _____.

4. A special bedtime ritual for younger children: Reading a favorite bedtime book or telling stories is a ritual that will be remembered most likely throughout their life. It's key to have a ritual with teens, too!

   Our bedtime ritual is: _____

   _____

5. Let your children help you: Parents sometimes inadvertently miss out on opportunities to forge closer relationships by not allowing their child to help them with various tasks and chores. Be prepared if they say "no." This isn't the same as the nonnegotiable chore that's been assigned to them.

I will ask my children to help me with the following:

_____

_____

_____

6. Play with your child: The key is to really play with your child. You truly are your child's favorite toy! Ask them, "Can I play with you?" "Want to play a video game?" or "Want to play a game of Uno (or some other board/card game they enjoy)?"

I will ask my child to play with me during these times of the day:

_____

_____

_____

7. Eat meals as a family: Families who eat together have better relationships. It gives you a forum for conversation. Be careful to be positive at dinnertime. It's not the time for discipline.

Our family will eat the following meals together:

_____

_____

_____

8. Seek out one-on-one opportunities often: Make time to spend with your child; if you have more than one child, allot time to spend with each. Even if it's just for 30 minutes, it counts. You could do an outing two times a month with just one of your children.

I will spend one-on-one time with each of my children in this way:

_____

_____

_____

9. Respect your child's choices: Let your child dress themself, and let your child be creative with hairstyles and choices of colors as long as it is appropriate. It does not reflect negatively on you if your child is wearing plaid and stripes. In fact, you might be raising a creative designer!

I will respect my child in the following ways:

_____

_____

_____

Make your children number one: Even when your life is stressful, make sure that you do steps 1 through 9. You are creating memories with your child, and who doesn't want to look back on their childhood and know how loved and important they were to their parents?

Why Did You Do That?

Have you ever asked your child, "Why did you do that?"

They may not be able to answer you right away, but there is actually a way to figure out why your child did that behavior.

Behavioral science has proven that each behavior is controlled by three big factors:

- Antecedence: which is a fancy word for what happened before the behavior

- Behavior: function of the behavior (the simple why)

- Consequence: what was the consequence of the behavior

Children's behavior can have different functions:

1. *Attention.* Very often both adults and children do things to get attention. It is important to remember that attention is attention. If your child is seeking attention and you are yelling at them, yes, they got attention!

2. *Tangible.* This is something physical that you get out of a behavior. A toddler may get a toy by pointing to it, or get a cup of milk by saying "milk."

3. *Escape/Avoidance.* These are two sides of the same coin: either escaping from or avoiding a situation that we do not like. I may slow down if I see a police officer to avoid a ticket, and my husband may take the trash out to escape my continual nagging. In the case of children, the escape/avoid behaviors very often present themselves in the school setting when the child wants to avoid a subject they don't like or that is too difficult for them.

4. *Sensory function.* This is when we do something for sensory reasons. A good example would be covering your ears when noise gets to be too much. In most extreme cases, self-injuries are very often a form of sensory stimulation.

So why does the function of the behavior matter? Well, if you can figure out the function of the behavior, you can provide your child what they are after in a desirable, positive way. If your child is seeking attention, you may teach them to ask for attention by saying, "Mom, can you please play with me?" The positive attention they will get this way will replace the not-so-good behaviors that we are trying to avoid.

There are two consequences that a behavior can have: (1) reinforcement and (2) punishment. They both occur right after the behavior (the sooner the better) but have an opposite effect on the FUTURE behavior. Reinforcement increases the behavior, and punishment decreases the behavior.

There is a common misconception about positive reinforcement and negative reinforcement. The positive and negative phrases have nothing to do with the emotional value assigned to each consequence. A positive reinforcement means that something has been ADDED to the environment after a behavior and that behavior has also INCREASED. Negative reinforcement means that something has been TAKEN AWAY from the environment and that behavior has also INCREASED. So in both cases of positive and negative reinforcement the behavior has increased.

Giving a child a cookie is an example of positive reinforcement only if the child is more likely to do what we rewarded him for (the behavior we are trying to encourage has increased) with the said cookie. If I stop nagging my husband (that is, the behavior of me nagging has been taken away) after he takes the trash out and his behavior of taking the trash out has increased, that would be an example of negative reinforcement.

Consequently, the same is true about punishment. Positive punishment means that something has been ADDED to the environment and the behavior has DECREASED, and negative punishment means something has been TAKEN AWAY from the environment and the behavior has DECREASED. Taking a phone away is an example of negative punishment only if the child does less of whatever we were punishing him for. If I add chores to the child's list after he misbehaves and the child then misbehaves less, that would be an example of positive punishment.

The two important things to remember about consequence are the fact that punishment teaches you what not to do, but it does not teach you what to do; and also, that punishment/reinforcement are defined by the person who we put the consequence on. If a child does not like playing with friends, grounding that child at home probably will be reinforcing—even though in the eyes of the parent the intent was punishment.

The last component that controls our own and our child's behavior are the antecedents. The antecedent is the environment or change in the environment that occurs or changes prior to a behavior. We can change behavior by changing a preexisting environment. There are two types of antecedents. One increases the effectiveness of reinforcement or makes something more desirable (for example when you are thirsty you want water), the other decreases the effectiveness of a reinforcement (if you just drank a bottle of juice you probably will not be interested in water). By noticing what is happening in the child's environment before the behavior we can look for patterns and discover triggers. Changing those will change the behavior itself.

By Karolina Labreque, PhD

Three Keys to Magical Connection: Stop. Look. Listen.

There are three keys to magical connections between parents and children. Use this easy-to-remember formula to be present with your child in times of need.

The first key is: **STOP**

We are in a world of distractions and the noise is deafening at times. As parents, we often forget that our "busy" can communicate abandonment, or worse, rejection, to our child's heart. Everything else can wait.

The second key is: **LOOK**

What do you see? Really see? Children have a way of bidding for our hearts and minds, our smiles and our time. Every bid they make, whether with a sweet little voice or an outburst of anger or frustration—it's a bid for YOU! "Do you see me?"

The third key is: **LISTEN**

Now you are engaged. Your calm voice, your tender eyes, and your open heart are ready to hear all the details that your little one is longing to tell you. Stay, *especially* when your child is upset. Stay until all the words tumble out into your welcoming, attentive space. Listen with rapt attention. Feeling loved is about feeling heard and understood.

Your "Magical Connection" checklist:

- ✓ Move quickly toward the upset with a calm voice.
- ✓ Get down to eye level to be sure they see your loving face.
- ✓ Touch them or hold them while you listen and console.
- ✓ Wait while all the words tumble out.
- ✓ Go with them to solve the problem that caused the tears.
- ✓ Assure them you are "with" them with smiles and hugs.

STOP. What keeps you from stopping your personal activity to give your full attention to your young child who is in distress, protesting, or demanding attention? Examples may be electronic devices, personal tasks, competing schedules, etc.

LOOK. What do you see in your child's eyes, their facial expression, and their way of asking for your attention? Do they seem overwhelmed, fearful, sad, excited, frustrated, delighted, or something else?

LISTEN. How can you assure your child that they have your full attention and that you will stay with them, calm them, and solve their upset every time? Will you use soft words, hugs, eye contact, touch, or something else?

By Myrna L. Hill, MA, LMFT

Movement Motivation & Plan

Ages: 5-12

Instructions:

Help your children understand how physical activity can empower them to accomplish other activities they like to do.

Complete the questions below with each one of your children. Encourage them to answer in their own words, but provide them with help, possibilities, and support as needed.

1. What activity or activities do you enjoy doing the most?

_____

2. How important to you is it that you do this activity well? (Rate on a scale of 1–5, with 1 being not at all and 5 being incredibly important.) _____

3. How can physical activity help you do the activities you enjoy even better? Here's a list to get you started. Circle all that apply. Be sure to add your own ideas to the list as well.

   - Encourages proper growth and development
   - Develops fine and gross motor skills
   - Builds strong bones and muscles
   - Increases energy
   - Encourages a healthy metabolism
   - Develops balance and coordination
   - Develops flexibility, endurance, and strength
   - Builds self-esteem
   - Improves concentration, thinking, and focuses attention
   - Encourages a mind-body connection
   - Relieves anxiety
   - Promotes sleep
   - Other _____

Once your child has answered these questions, create a plan. Work together to agree to a window(s) of time each day that each one of your children will put their device down and move. The goal is to schedule a window(s) that totals 60 minutes per day of activity, preferably before device time.

Tip: Print a weekly calendar for each child and write down the time each day. Keep that time protected as much as possible. Give your children a star each day they meet their goal!

Activity

Who's Got Your Back?

Ages: 13+

Purpose: To help adolescents identify the people who support them in their lives.

Who has your back? Who will be there for you? If you don't have a support system, feeling all alone can be very overwhelming.

Having a support system is especially important if you are creating change in your life. Making a commitment to improve is a giant step. Most of us have the best intentions, start out full force, and then kaput! It's over and done, and we feel like a failure. The reason? Lack of support.

One of the most important discoveries I have made in the past 10 years is that "support equals success." Every endeavor I have made in business or in my personal life has been filled with supportive friends, mentors, and the people who love me and I love back.

Instructions:

Make of a list of the people in your life who you can count on. If you come up short, make another list of potential new people to cultivate relationships with. Then reach out and connect.

People who support me:

1. _____

2. _____

3. _____

4. _____

5. _____

People who potentially would support me:

1. _____

2. _____

3. _____

4. _____

5. _____

Creating Memories for Life

Purpose: To create rituals and structure that provide children and adolescents with positive childhood memories. This can be presented in family therapy sessions and then be completed at home.

Materials:

- Timer
- Pens

Instructions:

Any time is a great time to put family rituals into place. Rituals are things that you do over and over again. It could be that you eat outdoors or that you take a walk together after dinner; or it might be that you go camping or take some type of family vacation together or visit relatives. It doesn't matter what you do or if it costs money or is free—what matters most is the time together. This is fairly easy to make happen with some children, but how do you entice children with special needs and tweens and teens to participate in family time?

During your family meeting, brainstorm a list of things that your children want to do and enjoy doing. Challenge them to come up with at least 10 ideas. You can even use a timer to make it fun. Let your children know that some activities can cost money, but that you want them to think of as many ideas as possible that are free. You can give ideas as examples, such as playing a game on Friday nights after dinner or making a home movie with your phone.

As you brainstorm with your children, be conscious of their developmental stage. This is meant to be fun and not a setup for your family to become frustrated or to have a meltdown. If your children's behavior gets out of control, make an effort to correct and teach rather than punish or send them out of the room.

Here are a few suggestions to get your creative juices flowing:

- Set the table with a cloth and your best dishes once a week and make a certain element of the meal the same (favorite dessert, special side, etc.).
- During summer, once a week take a picnic to the park or beach for dinner.
- During winter, set one night a week aside as family movie night.
- On Saturday or Sunday mornings, sleep a bit later and have brunch together.
- Take pictures of the table set, the picnic, and all the activities that you do together.

Do these same activities over and over again year in and year out (of course variations on the same themes is okay too), and you have created wonderful family memories for you and your kids.

Look at Me!

Ages: 5–9

Purpose: To increase eye contact in children with Opposition Defiant Disorder, Attention Deficit Hyperactivity Disorder and/or Autism Spectrum Disorder.

Materials:

- Timer
- Stickers
- Paper
- Pen

Instructions:

1. Tell the child or adolescent that you are going to play the "staring game."

2. Set the timer and see who can stare the longest (most people can't stare more than five seconds). Stop and ask, "What was that like?"

3. Place a small sticker between your eyebrows and ask the child to look at that. Stop and ask, "What was that like?"

4. Next, try the triangle approach: Look at one eye for five seconds, the second eye for five seconds, and the mouth for five seconds. Stop and ask, "What was that like?"

5. Continue practicing with the child to encourage eye contact. You'll notice over time that the child will become more and more comfortable.

Inspiration

Uncover Your Parenting Brilliance with CLARITY

Connect with your child on a regular basis. This helps to establish a stronger relationship and fosters more cooperation. Set aside a specific time for a special activity or use everyday routines (e.g., mealtime, bedtime) to connect. During this special time, your child is the primary focus. Put away any electronics or other distractions.

Listen to your child with an open heart and mind. Your goal is to gain insight and understanding rather than offering your opinion. Get down to your child's level and be fully present. Validate your child's feelings. Ask questions to gain further understanding. Ask permission before sharing your own thoughts.

Accept your child's temperament and individual differences. Appreciate the gifts your child has to offer. Learn to look at challenges through a new lens.

Respond to your child's needs rather than to the behaviors. Behavior is communication. In the heat of the moment, look beyond what you see or hear and consider what's underneath it. Perhaps your child is feeling sad, angry, afraid, humiliated, powerless, frustrated, tired, or hungry. Acknowledge the feeling and support the need (e.g., validation, attention, comfort, power, food, sleep).

Invite your child's help in finding solutions to problems. Your child will feel a sense of empowerment and is more likely to do things differently when involved in the problem solving.

Trust in your and your child's abilities. It takes time to learn new ways of doing things. Trust that with time and the right tools and support, skills can be learned and things can improve.

Your needs matter too. It's hard to be the parent that you want to be when you feel depleted emotionally and physically. Model for your child what self-care looks like. Take time for yourself on a regular basis.

By Jessica Silverman, Parenting Coach

For CLARITY

Make a list of activities with your child that you'd like to do together (e.g., play a game, have a pillow fight, take a hike, read a book, make a meal).

1. _____

2. _____

3. _____

The way we communicate with our children influences how they communicate with others and with us. Communication is both verbal and nonverbal. Be mindful of your body language, facial expressions, tone of voice, and language used.

Model how to be a good listener by making eye contact, restating what was said, and validating feelings. Talk less and listen more when your child is communicating. A child is more likely to open up to someone who listens to what they have to say without judgment.

Make a list of your child's gifts (reframe the language that you use to describe your child: e.g., relentless becomes persistent; nosy becomes curious; wild becomes adventurous).

1. _____

2. _____

3. _____

View behaviors with compassion and curiosity. Consider the feeling driving the behavior, the unmet need or skill that needs to be developed.

Brainstorm solutions to problems with your child. Find a solution that you both agree with. Try it for at least a week and reevaluate as necessary. See mistakes as opportunities to learn and grow. None of us is perfect. Be kind to your child and yourself.

Make a list of activities that bring you joy and peace (e.g., meditation, journaling, a walk outside, a bubble bath, lunch with a friend). Make self-care a priority.

1. _____

2. _____

3. _____

By Jessica Silverman, Parenting Coach

Family Meetings:
Run Your Home Like a Business

Is it difficult to get your family together? Are mealtimes chaotic? Are you stuck doing all the chores? Is your family operating individually and not as a team? Do members of your family have constant miscommunications? Is your teenager disengaged from the family, isolating in his or her room, always at a friend's house, never home or never available? If so, do you want to increase communication, have everyone be on the same page, and plan fun and enjoyable times together?

Family meetings are a great way to improve communication with your children and have an organized, enjoyable, and meaningful family life.

A family meeting provides you with the forum to pull your family together, communicate the week's events/responsibilities, and make family decisions about household chores or even planning a vacation!

How to set up your first family meeting:

1. Pick a time and place (e.g., the living room on Saturday or Sunday morning at 11 a.m.).

2. Tell your family that the meeting will be no longer than 30 minutes.

3. At the start of the first meeting ask someone in the family to volunteer to take notes and someone to watch the clock.

4. Let family members know that everyone will be taking turns with notetaking and running the meetings.

5. Let them know that this meeting is mandatory (important decisions will be made; if they don't show, then they won't have a say).

The following page gives a sample agenda for your first family meeting.

Your First Family Meeting

Introduce the concept of the family meeting (why do you want to have family meetings?).

  a. Set a time: Meetings will be held every Sunday at 11 a.m. for no longer than 30 minutes.

  b. Everyone is expected to be there.

  c. If a member cannot be there, explain that the meeting notes will be kept in a notebook available for all family members to review.

Establish rules and procedures for the meetings.

  a. One person talks at a time.

  b. All suggestions are welcome.

  c. No judgment; no one is wrong.

Explain that a blank agenda will be posted on the fridge where family members can fill in topics to be discussed at the next meeting.

Come up with something fun to do after the meeting and do it.

A family meeting does not work if:

  1. They are held at the dinner table or in the car.

  2. Kids complain or whine.

  3. Parents use the meetings to discipline.

How to have the best family meeting on the block:

  1. Start the meeting with compliments. Tell your children all the great things that you noticed about them in the past week. Even if you are at a loss, find something positive to say anyway! Then ask the children to say positive things to the other family members and so forth.

  2. During the meeting make sure that everyone gets to say how they feel.

  3. Make sure you reach a resolution during the discussion.

  4. Record and document your family meetings and keep the notes available to everyone.

  5. At the beginning of the next meeting, review the notes from the previous meeting.

  6. Important: Always end with something fun which helps family members feel good, like a group hug, game, or family ritual.

Blended Families and Discipline:
"You're Not My Dad! You Can't Tell Me What To Do!"

Second marriages and other adult unions bring up issues for kids. You may have noticed that the kids are acting out or retreating to their rooms more often. It is a good idea for you and your future spouse to decide how you will handle discipline before you live together or marry. No matter if you are a new step-parent or you have been hitting your head against the wall for what seems like years trying to get peace at home, take a deep breath and try these five steps.

1. **Step-parent as Uncle/Aunt, Friend, Coach, etc.**

   As a new step-parent, you have your job cut out for you. In the beginning, take a step back and see yourself as needing to connect with the kids rather than disciplining them. Let the child's or teenager's biological parent handle the correcting, reprimanding, etc. Work on creating a close relationship with the new child/teen in your life. Do this until the child/teen has accepted you. Even if you have been blended for years, take a step back.

2. **Stay Neutral**

   Don't get pulled into a debate between your spouse and their child/teen about a behavior. Let your spouse handle the situation. Only join in when/if your spouse asks for your help.

3. **Get a Hobby**

   Allow your spouse/partner to have "alone/special" time with their child/teen. The kids need this and your marital relationship needs this, too. There is plenty of time for family time. Let the kids know that you are not taking their mom or dad away from them.

4. **Offer Help**

   Offer your help to the child/teen in areas of homework, sports, problem solving. Even if they turn you down, don't retreat. Let the kids know that you are available if they have a problem or need help.

5. **Family Meeting**

   Once you have bonded with the children you can begin sharing some of the discipline with your spouse. With your spouse, set up a few house rules and consequences, and share these with the kids during your family meeting. This takes you out of the middle. It also makes you and your spouse a united front.

How to Write a Family Mission Statement

Ages: 4-18

Purpose: To help foster communication, peace, and harmony at home. To help teach children/teens accountability, planning and organizational skills.

Instructions:

1. Start with a family meeting.

2. Explain that you would like to come up with a family mission statement, and by having one there will be less confusion about what your day-to-day and long-term goals as a family are. This will help you, as a family, stay on track to help the house run smoothly daily and ensure cooperation, kindness, and compassion.

3. Get the kids to talk about what makes your family special and take notes. (For instance: we are funny, we like to go camping, we like to go to the movies, we like celebrating, volunteering, etc.)

4. Now come up with sentences that reflect those values that are within the specialness of the family. Continue to edit the statement until the family is in agreement and all members feel that they had a part in its creation.

5. Print out the mission statement, frame it, and then hang it in a place for all to see.

6. When family members notice that the family is drifting from the values, suggest that the family members reread the statement.

7. Once or twice a year have a special family meeting to go over the mission statement and update it accordingly.

Example:

"The Jones family loves to spend time together, whether we are celebrating birthdays or just eating dinner together. We love to make each other laugh and are respectful to one another and strive to be considerate at all times. We understand that we all make mistakes and that we can learn from these; therefore, we take responsibility for our own actions. We believe that it is important to be involved in our community and help others who are less fortunate."

The worksheet on the following page will help to get you started.

Family Mission Statement

We the _____ family, love to _____

_____

_____

_____

We value _____

_____

_____

_____

We understand _____

_____

_____

_____

We believe _____

_____

_____

_____

Therapist Activity

You Are Your Child's Favorite Toy

Purpose: Teaching parents how to play with their children and increase their bond.

Instructions:

Invite parents/caregivers into the play therapy room and try these ideas:

1. Remind parents that playing with kids doesn't have to be long and involved. It can be in 5- to 10-minute spurts.

2. Have the parent/caregiver read a short book or poem aloud to the child.

3. Tell the parent/caregiver to ask the child, "Can I play with you?" In kid-speak, this means, "I like you."

4. Encourage adults to always approach children rather than having children approach them for play. It always works out better if you don't have to say "no," because in kids-speak, it means, "I don't like you."

5. Sit with a child and watch him or her play without talking. Listen and watch—you will be surprised with the stories and information that they will share while playing.

6. Draw on a piece of paper and cover up what you are doing. Kids are curious. They will pry your arm away to see, and when they do, you can ask, "Would you like a turn?"

Technology

Media and digital devices are an integral part of our world today. The benefits of these devices, if used moderately and appropriately, can broaden experience, promote creativity, and connect us to others. Despite this, research has shown that face-to-face time with family, friends, and teachers is essential in promoting children's learning and healthy development. Parents, teachers, and caregivers have a responsibility to ensure that the face-to-face time is favored over time on devices. Adults can model healthy alternatives by spending time reading, exploring a hobby, having friends over and enjoying outdoor activities.

The contracts and agreements found here provide structure and conversation to keep kids safe, alternatives to device usage, and a look at ourselves as role models in our fast-paced and ever-changing world.

Get Outside

Years ago, it was common to send kids out to "play." (I was certainly sent out for hours even in the coldest weather.) But, sadly, the world has changed and parents are afraid to let children roam unsupervised. "They might get snatched!" Or maybe your neighbors will judge you, "That parent doesn't supervise her children!"

In 2005, the manufacturers of Persil laundry detergent did a survey called "Dirt is good: The 33 things you should do before you're 10."

Here are some of them: (Have you done these things? Have your kids?)

- Roll down a grassy bank
- Make a mud pie
- Catch frogs
- Build a sand castle
- Climb a tree
- Make snow angels
- Take part in a scavenger hunt
- Camp out in the yard
- Feed a farm animal
- Find some worms
- Ride a bike through a mud puddle
- Make and fly a kite
- Find 10 different leaves
- Plant a tree

These activities don't cost a cent, provide plenty of fresh air and tire kids out, which helps kids sleep for more hours. According to studies, kids who sleep more are less likely to have a weight problem. This is a wonderful start to a full, active, healthy life that you can provide for your children.

Inspiration

Expanding Childhood Beyond the Digital World

There is a myriad of concerns when it comes to children's exposure to technology. One that's not up for debate is that increased use of electronic devices often leads to decreased physical activity. But daily physical activity is vital to both a child's development and to their long-term health.

You can use several effective strategies to encourage your children to close the screen and get moving. The key component that runs through all of these strategies is to encourage your child's enjoyment in physical activity. The more comfortable they feel and the more fun they have, the more likely they'll be to put their devices down and move their bodies—with less arguing and less stress on you.

Tips for Engaging Your Child in Physical Activity

- Increase your children's awareness of why it's important to be physically active. Help them make the connection between activity and feeling strong and energized. Offer examples of what they can accomplish when they feel strong and healthy that are relevant to their life.

- Focus on what your child can do with their time, rather than what they can't do (e.g., use their device). Use examples that appeal to your children, such as play outside, play with friends, go for a bike ride, etc.

- Give your child a chance to experiment to see what activities appeal to them. All children need the time and space to experiment with different activities until they figure out what they really like to do and would choose over electronics. Children who feel physically awkward or uncomfortable being physically active may need some extra help in finding activities that they enjoy. This is when technology can be helpful, rather than detrimental. If they'd feel more open to doing an exercise video by themselves in the comfort of home rather than playing ball with a group of kids, try searching on YouTube for kids' workouts, kids' yoga, kids' dance videos, etc., or looking on Amazon for a DVD that they'd like to try.

- Schedule regular "family fun" days. Brainstorm a list of activities you can do as a family and let each child take turns picking the activity. Some ideas include:

  — Family kickball game

  — Backyard obstacle course

  — Living room dance party

  — Outdoor hike

  — Family workout video

  — Trip to an indoor adventure center

By Pamela Power, M.S.

Inspiration

Technology and Distractibility

Within the last decade or so technology has seen an even bigger boom than most of us could ever have imagined. Just as we were amazed at an astronaut landing on the moon in 1968, we baby boomers are blown away by computers, cell phones, and Twitter.

The impact of technology on children, tweens, and teens is astounding. Kids these days seem to breathe text messaging and other social media. No longer are kids giving out the home telephone number—in fact, many families don't even have a landline.

Some of this is good because we can contact our kids at will, but some aspects of this are also troubling:

- Looking at their phones hundreds of times a day=interrupted thought process.
- Conversations being interrupted to respond to a text message=not finishing sentences.
- Sleeping with phones=interrupted sleep.
- Phones at school=interruptions in class.
- Phones during homework=interrupted concentration.

An article in *USA Today* in August 2009, referred to a phenomenon called "Cultural Autism" with the use of cell phones and computer communication, which led to:

- Inability to express feelings or emotions face to face.
- Fear of using telephones to set up their own appointments.
- Inability to have face-to-face conversations.

Some solutions to this problem for you to consider this school year:

- Before you purchase your child's first cell phone, ask yourself, "Why am I doing this?" If it is because your child is begging you, saying that they cannot live without it and everyone else has one, think good and hard before you buy.
- Decide if your child/tween/teen really requires a cell phone while at school and if not, do not allow them to bring it.
- Consider making it a rule that cell phones are handed over to parents after school and returned when homework is completed; and also that cell phones are handed over to parents during the child's sleeping hours.

Cell phones will become a power struggle. There is no way around it. Having a system for controlling their use will ensure that your child grows up socially adept and with a mind that can focus on one thing at a time.

Cell phones are only one distraction, of course, and there are many more. Before your child/tween/teen starts school, take a look at the computer, video games, TV, etc. What do you need to do to help limit these distractions? And while you are at it, look at all of this for yourself as well.

Electronics Cost Money

Ages: 5-11

Purpose: To teach financial responsibility and to control use of electronics at home.

Materials:

- Quarters

Instructions:

1. Because you are paying the bills for all things "electronic," explain to the kids that they will have to pay to use these things as well. Each child will be given a set amount of coins at the beginning of the week that they must allocate for using the electronics. When the money runs out, that's it for the week.

2. You can offer an incentive that if there is leftover money at the end of the week, they can spend it at the grocery store on a special treat when you go shopping.

3. First, determine how much of each electronic you would approve of on average per week. If your child is permitted to watch one hour of TV and to use the computer for one hour a day, multiply that times seven, for a total of 14 hours of total electronics per week. If every hour costs 50 cents, then that is a total of $7 per week.

4. Consider breaking down the available time into 30-minute intervals and providing quarters for payment.

Internet Use

1. I will not give out personal information such as my address, telephone number, parents' work address/telephone number, or the name and location of my school without my parents' permission.

2. I will tell my parents immediately if I come across any information that makes me feel uncomfortable or confused.

3. I will never agree to get together with someone I "meet" online without first checking with my parents. If my parents agree to the meeting, I will be sure that it is in a public place and bring my mother or father along.

4. I will go online when my parents say it's OK and limit my online time so that it doesn't interfere with chores, homework, or other activities.

5. I will not respond to any messages that are mean or in any way make me feel uncomfortable. It is not my fault if I get a message like that. If I do I will tell my parents right away.

6. I will work with my parents so that we can set up rules for going online. We will decide upon the time of day that I can be online, the length of time I can be online, and appropriate websites for me to visit. I will not access other sites or break these rules without their permission.

7. I will not give out my passwords to anyone (even my best friends) other than my parents.

8. I will check with my parents before downloading or installing software or apps or doing anything that could possibly hurt our devices or jeopardize my family's privacy.

9. I will be a good online citizen and not do anything that hurts other people or is against the law.

10. I will help my parents understand how to have fun and learn things online and teach them things about the internet, computers, and other technology. ☺

Child Signature: _____   Date: _____

Parent Signature: _____   Date: _____

Inspiration

10 Smartphone Rules for Kids

Use this as a cheat sheet to prepare yourself to speak with your child/teen about smartphone use. On page 228 there is a contract you can use to reach a mutual agreement.

Here's how to talk to your kids about smartphone use:

"We know that having this phone is not only a necessity, but it can be a good, fun, and useful tool. But don't forget that you live in the real world, not behind a screen or a camera.

"We want you to live a healthy and quality life, not a life concerned with how many 'followers' or 'likes' you have. Now, more than ever, it is important for you to remember that you must stand up for what is right, walk away from what is wrong, and ask us for help if you aren't sure. We promise not to judge you. And if you decide you don't need to engage with others on your phone, that's great too!

"You are responsible for using this phone appropriately, and as your parents we are ultimately responsible for your behavior. We will have access to your phone content, because it is our responsibility to ensure that you are communicating safely and respectfully. [This may change as your kids get older.]

"Please remember this: You will never get into trouble for reporting ANY suspicious behavior, as well as any behavior that scares or worries you. If you made a mistake, come tell us about it and we can deal with it. Do not try to hide it as that makes it worse."

10 Non-Negotiable Cell Phone Rules

1. Whose Phone Is This?

It is our phone. We paid for it. Essentially, we are loaning it to you. The main reasons you are receiving this phone are for communication with your parents and for personal safety (the ability to get help or assistance if you need it). This phone is not a toy.

The phone has a password so that no one can pick it up and use your apps, send emails on your behalf, update your status, etc. This password will be known by us at all times. The same applies for any app or email address that needs a password.

2. Appropriate Time Uses

Phone or text communication should not occur before 7:00 a.m. in the morning or after 8:00 p.m. on weekdays and 9:00 p.m. on weekends, unless you are communicating with parents or other adult family members. After 8:00 p.m. your phone should be turned off and charging in my room. *(Again, these times are negotiable for older kids.)*

3. Etiquette

If the phone rings, answer it. It is a phone. Say hello, use your manners. Do not ever ignore a phone call if the screen reads "Mom" or "Dad." Not ever.

4. Common Sense

No taking videos or pictures of unsuspecting people. No videos or pictures in the name of humor at the expense of another human, siblings and parents included. Always get permission to post.

Do not take photos of other people's embarrassing situations. If someone falls and hurts themselves the correct reaction is to help, not to put it on YouTube. You would not like your face plastered all over YouTube unknowingly.

5. Cyber Bullying

The phone is not an excuse to be rude, hurtful, or mean. A text is the exact same thing as verbally saying it out loud. If you would not say something in person, do not text it with the phone.

Remember that text messages can be forwarded to many other people. You cannot get back a text message after sending it, and a message lives on long after you send it.

If other people are being mean and hurtful to someone on their phone, behave as you would in real life. Do not be part of the conversation. Report all bullying immediately.

If I check your phone, there should be nothing in there that I would be horrified to find. If you are not sure, ask yourself if you would be happy to say it out loud in the room with me listening … if there is a doubt—don't say it.

Be a good friend.

6. The Phone at Home

Basic courtesy applies. You know when it's acceptable to speak on the phone and when it's not. Same rule applies to texting. If we are having dinner, do not sit on your phone texting. That is just rude. Family time is golden, and just like Mom and Dad put away their phones, so will you.

No phone calls should be made or text messages sent during homework time.

7. Friending People

Never accept as a friend anyone you don't know personally. There are people who try to friend kids via mobile phone and social media apps. They can pretend to be your friend, but they are not. The "don't talk to strangers" rule applies for mobile phones too.

Never tell anyone where you live or where you are.

8a. XXX Behavior *(Decide how to approach this based on your child's age.)*

Do not, under any circumstances, take photos of your private parts or receive pictures of anyone else's private parts. This is known as Sexting.

This behavior could ruin your teenage/college/adult life. Cyberspace is vast and more powerful than you. And it is hard to make anything of this magnitude disappear—including a bad reputation.

As a rule, assume that any picture that you take or that someone takes of you with your phone will be on the front page of the newspaper and shown to everyone at school.

8b. XXX Content *(Also decide the language based on your child's age, but don't ignore this part.)*

The internet is full of inappropriate images and videos that can be accessed by mobile phones. You will stumble on it. Curious? Got questions? Superb! We are here to answer everything. What your friends tell you "they know" is nonsense and your phone is not the tool to find out. 99% of the time your friends will make stuff up to seem cool. Yes, it is going to be embarrassing to ask Mom and Dad. But we promise we will never mock the question or shy away from it and will give you the info you want.

9. The Care of Your Phone

If it falls into the toilet, smashes on the ground, or disappears, you are responsible for the replacement costs or repairs. Start thinking now about how you will earn that money, because chances are something will happen. Be prepared.

10. Final Comments About Your Phone and This Contract

It is a privilege, not a right, to own a cell phone. If there is a problem with content, a decision will be made based on what happened, not what you thought would happen. If at any time this tool is misused, we reserve the option of removing this phone from your care for a time to enable you to think about appropriate use of your cell phone.

By Sheryl Gould, Parenting Coach

Smartphone Usage

1. I understand that this phone is owned by my parents. The main reasons I am receiving this phone is to communicate with them, and for personal safety.

2. All of my passwords and usernames for my phone, apps, and email will be known by my parents at all times; and I won't be mad if they check my accounts.

3. Appropriate use times are __a.m. - ___p.m. on weekdays and __a.m. - __p.m. on weekends. At night my phone will be turned off and charged in an agreed upon place.

4. I will not use the phone during homework or mealtimes, or any other times we agree upon.

5. I will not take videos or pictures of people without their permission. I will not use videos or pictures of people because I think they're funny without permission.

6. I will never be mean or hurtful to someone in a text, post, or chat. I understand that once I hit send it is out in the world forever. Anyone can screenshot.

7. I will report bullying immediately.

8. I will never accept a friend request or chat request from someone I don't know in real life. I will never tell anyone where I live or post pictures of identifying places. I understand that someone who seems nice in a chat may not be who they say they are. The "Stranger Danger" rule applies here too.

9. I understand that I am responsible for losing or damaging my phone.

10. I understand that this contract represents trust between me and my parents, and if I break that trust by violating any of these rules, there will be consequences including, but not limited to, losing my phone privileges.

11. I will not, under any circumstances, take photos of myself not fully clothed or my private parts, or receive pictures of anyone else's private parts. This is illegal.

12. I understand that any picture I take or that someone else takes of me can be screenshotted and shared with anyone in the world at any time.

13. The internet is full of inappropriate images and videos that can be accessed by mobile phones. I understand that the images I find online do not necessarily represent "real life." Additionally, what my friends tell me "they know" is nonsense and my phone is not the tool to find out. 99% of the time my friends make stuff up to seem cool. If I am curious about things, or have questions, my parents are here to answer everything. I understand that it might be embarrassing to ask my parents. But they promise they will never joke or shy away from my questions, and they will give me the info I want.

Child/Teen Signature: _____ Date: _____

Parent Signature: _____Date: _____

Parent Self-Care

Many parents run on empty, and proper self-care is sometimes overlooked while caring for kids, keeping a house, and working full-time. Physical, emotional, intellectual, and spiritual self-care will keep even the most overwhelmed parent refreshed, energized, and ready to handle the next challenging situation.

- *Physical self-care* includes exercise, sleep, nutrition, and breaks such as long walks alone, a massage, or a relaxing cup of tea.
- *Emotional self-care* includes spending time with friends, spending time alone, prioritizing obligations, bringing creativity into your day, humor, dates with a partner/spouse, or an evening out with friends.
- *Intellectual self-care* includes reading, writing, pursuing a hobby, listening to music, and learning something new.
- *Spiritual self-care* may include religious practices, meditating, volunteering, and contributing to a cause you believe in.

Raising kids with mental health diagnoses, challenging behaviors, and other family issues is stressful. Discovering how to take time for yourself and knowing when you need a break is essential in maintaining a positive connection with your kids. You know the saying, "Put your oxygen mask on first"? Well, it's true for raising children as well. This section is full of tips and strategies for you to use yourself.

Inspiration

One Perfect Moment

Most parents and educators dream of one perfect day with their kids; one day during which there is no hitting, kicking, screaming, and no "You can't make me!" Homework is completed without nagging, teeth are brushed without reminding, dinnertime is filled with wonderful conversations, and when you tuck your angels into bed there are many smiles.

Oh, to all be so happy and relaxed! I remember wishing for this many times. As I look back on the last 10 years, when I was raising my kids (a portion of which I was a single parent), I don't think that there ever was one perfect day.

I am quite amazed that I could do it all: working full-time, dinner on the table six of seven nights, lunches made, cookies baked, homework, bath time, reading to the kids, doctors and dentist appointments, shopping, cleaning, Little League, dance, Girl Scouts, selling cookies and wrapping paper, religious school, birthday parties, school plays, chicken pox, stomach flu, strep, up all night with sick kids, friends for the kids, sledding, ice skating, swimming lessons, holiday shopping, holidays in general, snow days, planning summers, planning and making vacations happen, finding sitters, making time for me and my interests, taking care of me (exercising, eating well, etc.), and being totally, totally, flexible!

What I did have were many, many perfect moments, and these are the moments I cherished then and remember today. How would you like more perfect moments (*perfect* meaning that you are doing everything you can be to the parent you want to be)? I am going to share my simple but effective secrets with you:

- Time is a commodity: I planned, planned, and planned.
- We shut off the TV Sunday night through Thursday nights (more time together, no arguing about what to watch or when to go to bed).
- I had a sitter, a backup sitter, and another backup sitter.
- I traded with other moms and dads for free time.
- I cooked on Sundays for the whole week.
- I made all lunches on Sundays.
- I learned to say "no" to a lot of people.
- I did not involve my kids in more than two after-school activities each week (preferably just one).
- Piano lessons were given at our house (no driving and waiting).
- We had a basketball hoop at our house (I knew where the kids were).
- We had family time, games, puzzles, and laughter.
- And when I felt overwhelmed, I asked for help from friends, relatives, and experts.

Inspiration

Emotional Intelligence & Parenting

Let's talk honestly. Sometimes your kid acts out and you just want to flip your lid. Other times, your kid is just being a kid but he's aggravating you to no end because you're working with limited patience and an abundance of stress. In either case, you might find yourself losing your temper or snapping at your child. That's normal. Many parents wouldn't blame you for it. But is it the most helpful way to respond to the situation? Probably not.

When we're overcome with emotions like anger, frustration, or sadness, we often lose the ability to empathize and connect with our child. But during stressful encounters or times of conflict, empathy and connection are actually what they need the most.

This workbook is a great resource to help you and your child develop the tools to cope with the overwhelming emotions and challenging situations that are part of life. But your ability to use the tools will be somewhat limited if you aren't first aware of your emotions and how they're influencing your actions and behaviors. That's why we're talking about *emotional intelligence* (EQ). If you don't have the EQ or self-awareness to know when to pick up which tool, then the application of these tools won't be as effective. EQ gives you access to choice. By increasing your EQ, you will increase your ability to choose the right tool for the circumstances. You will be able to intentionally respond, rather than automatically react, to difficult parenting situations.

Increasing your own EQ will help your child, as well. By watching you function from a space of self-awareness, your child will learn from you how to increase his or her own EQ. They'll observe you using the tools in action, and will intuitively begin to learn how to use the tools for themselves, too!

What Does Emotional Intelligence Mean?

Google defines EQ as "the capacity to be aware of, control and express one's emotions, and to handle interpersonal relationships judiciously and empathetically." In lay terms, EQ is basically just the ability to identify and manage your own emotions, and understand and connect to the emotions of others. It means not only knowing that your frustration is rising, but also knowing what to do about it. It means not only knowing how your child is feeling when she's upset, but also knowing how to connect with her through her feelings. From this perspective, I actually deem EQ to be the foundation of effective parenting. It gives you the ability to choose in the moment how you want to show up, rather than letting your automatic reactions take over.

The Four Factors of Emotional Intelligence

Being emotionally intelligent doesn't mean having awareness in one specific area. Four critical factors make up EQ. They are:

AWARENESS: I accurately recognize and acknowledge my emotions.

EXPRESSION: I have self-control when sharing my feelings.

UNDERSTANDING: I accurately recognize and acknowledge the feelings of others.

CONNECTION: I have an authentic, emotional bond between myself and others.

When you read these four factors, you might feel like you have a lot of EQ in one area—maybe understanding—and less EQ in another area. That's normal. But healthy EQ strives to have balance across all four factors, so that's what we're working toward.

It's also normal for your EQ to ebb and flow, depending on circumstances. I like to think of EQ as a spectrum, rather than a black-and-white issue. That is to say, it's not that we either have it or we don't have it—it comes down to *how much* EQ we have at that moment. And since EQ is fluid, we might have more awareness on some days and less on others. The goal isn't to be flawless— no amount of EQ will make you the perfect parent, because there's no such thing. The goal is to function with as much awareness as you can as often as possible.

Assessing Your EQ

To increase your EQ, you first have to learn how to assess it. This helps us know where we're strong and where we need to build some EQ muscle.

Here's a simple way to assess your level of EQ. In each of the four areas (Awareness, Expression, Understanding, and Connection) rate yourself using this scale:

Reactive – you let your reactivity determine how you show up, you aren't able to empathize with how others are feeling (including your child), and you cut off connection from others.

Numb – you aren't connected to any feeling at the moment, have checked out completely, and avoid connecting with others.

Confused – you are able to identify your feelings, but you're not sure what to do about them or how to connect or empathize with others.

Insightful – you are aware of your feelings and that you can choose how you express your emotions, but you aren't sure what would be most helpful for the situation.

Present – you are fully aware of how you're feeling and of all of the choices you have in that moment, you are able to empathize and connect with others, and are comfortable choosing a response you think is the most helpful for the situation.

I want to emphasize that cultivating your EQ is a lifelong learning experience. We can never build too much! To jump-start your learning, I've created the following exercises to help you assess and build your EQ over time. The first exercise is meant to be completed right now and will help you identify your baseline score in each area. It will also give you specific "Dares" to increase your EQ in that area. "Dares" are challenges to take you out of your comfort zone and to give you a new perspective and experience on an emotional trigger.

The second exercise can be completed when you are feeling upset or overwhelmed, and will help you identify your "triggered" score in a difficult situation. It will also ask you to identify specific things you can do right then to help you become more emotionally intelligent during that specific situation. This is where you will want to call on a specific dare from Exercise #1 and the activities in this workbook to help you deal with stress in the moment.

EXERCISE #1

Take a few minutes right now to complete the worksheet "Assessment Sheet for Your Baseline EQ" on the following page. This will show you where your EQ strengths are and will also highlight the areas you might need to work on. After you've completed the score, look through the recommended dares for each EQ factor. Try out as many of them as you can, and note which ones felt helpful to you.

This process needs to be done while you're calm, and not overwhelmed with emotions. This will facilitate building your tools in advance so that you have these skills to call upon when you're in the middle of an emotionally-charged situation.

EXERCISE #2

This exercise is designed to be used when you find yourself in a frustrating situation or overwhelmed with emotions. Use the worksheet "Using EQ During a Difficult Situation" on page 235, and circle the accurate state for each of the four critical areas. Then follow the action steps to help you connect with your EQ in the moment.

Create a habit of using Exercise #2 and you will notice that you will develop the ability to use these tools automatically.

After you complete each exercise, use the "Reflection" worksheet on page 236.

By Diane Shrock, LMFT

Assessment Sheet for Your Baseline EQ

AWARENESS:

I accurately recognize and acknowledge my emotions.

YOUR BASELINE STATE:

1. Reactive
2. Numb
3. Confused
4. Insightful
5. Present

*To increase your <u>awareness</u>, **Dare** yourself to:*

- Walk or sit a little taller than normal.
- Say YES to something that scares you (and it's okay to start with something small).
- Write down five emotions you feel every day for a week.

EXPRESSION:

I have self-control when sharing my feelings.

YOUR BASELINE STATE:

1. Reactive
2. Numb
3. Confused
4. Insightful
5. Present

*To increase your <u>expression</u>, **Dare** yourself to:*

- Think something negative and DON'T say it aloud.
- Say something kind to yourself right now, even if you don't feel like it.
- Tell somebody how you're really feeling, even if it's uncomfortable.

UNDERSTANDING:

I accurately recognize and acknowledge the feelings of others.

YOUR BASELINE STATE:

1. Reactive
2. Numb
3. Confused
4. Insightful
5. Present

*To increase your <u>understanding</u>, **Dare** yourself to:*

- Listen to someone else without preparing an answer.

CONNECTION:

I have an authentic emotional bond between myself and others.

YOUR BASELINE STATE:

1. Reactive
2. Numb
3. Confused
4. Insightful
5. Present

*To increase your <u>connection</u>, **Dare** yourself to:*

- Compliment the next person you make eye contact with.
- Send a text to someone that says: "Just thinking of you today."
- Think of a moment you could trust someone or something.

By Diane Shrock, LMFT

Using EQ During a Difficult Situation

AWARENESS:

I accurately recognize and acknowledge my emotions.

YOUR CURRENT STATE:

1. Reactive
2. Numb
3. Confused
4. Insightful
5. Present

ACTION STEP:

List three emotions you're feeling right now:

-
-
-

EXPRESSION:

I have self-control when sharing my feelings.

YOUR CURRENT STATE:

1. Reactive
2. Numb
3. Confused
4. Insightful
5. Present

ACTION STEP:

List three healthy ways you can express your feelings right now:

-
-
-

UNDERSTANDING:

I accurately recognize and acknowledge the feelings of others.

YOUR CURRENT STATE:

1. Reactive
2. Numb
3. Confused
4. Insightful
5. Present

ACTION STEP:

List three emotions your child is feeling right now (if you don't know, ask!):

-
-
-

CONNECTION:

I have an authentic emotional bond between myself and others.

YOUR CURRENT STATE:

1. Reactive
2. Numb
3. Confused
4. Insightful
5. Present

ACTION STEP:

List three steps you can take to connect with your child right now:

-
-
-

By Diane Shrock, LMFT

Reflection

It's always a great idea to reflect after using the EQ exercises. Take a few minutes to write down your experiences.

- What helped you?

- What do you want to try next time?

- How do you think your EQ can be used moving forward?

By Diane Shrock, LMFT

Attention Moms: Identify Your Overwhelm

Landing yourself in this book and in this chapter tells me something about you. You are obviously committed to seeing your children grow up to be capable and responsible adults. You love them dearly and want them to live their dream. Yet there is another part of you that is feeling the under current of overwhelm as you are parenting in today's world.

You're working a job or running your own business. You really want to make a difference in today's world and contribute something meaningful. And you want to be a great momma.

You are running a household and caring for all the activities and extracurricular activities that go along with what is viewed as necessary in our culture. It's no surprise that you feel overwhelmed with what appears to be necessary. You know that something really needs to change, yet putting your finger on what that is can be daunting, so you go on keeping the status quo.

Days and months later you're in the same place, but a little more tired and frustrated. You may be putting on that cheery face and looking like all is well, yet deep inside you are coping with exhaustion, guilt, and a sense of unhappiness because in some way—although you are doing it all—you feel like you are not quite measuring up. And you're silently crumbling under the pressure:

- The pressure of trying to be someone or something you are not.
- The pressure of trying to fit yourself into someone else's (often outdated) model of parenting.

It's simply not working for you. You are here with your own mission and purpose. You are a gift to yourself and your children and the world. However, this requires authenticity with yourself first. It means that you must first understand and embrace who you are and why you are here—how you roll in life. Gaining this wisdom and acceptance creates a whole new energy of alignment that is vital to you and your parenting. It starts with you because you cannot pass on to your children what you do not have.

The truth is, that as you stop fighting against who you are, and stop being what society and your environment says you should be, you will discover what is right for you and your family and you will find yourself in peace.

The truth is, you need to live in harmony. You need to know yourself, and I mean really know who you are. You need to see your gifts, purpose, and the path you are here to walk.

Your inner self has a map, and learning to read that map affords you the opportunity to follow it and move into alignment with yourself. And this is what equips you to do the same for your children.

When you are living in harmony, it impacts everything:

- The choices you make

- How you parent

- Where you find fulfillment and meaning in life

- And how happy you are

When you live in your truth, you'll have the confidence in yourself that you're doing a good job raising your children.

You will trust your decisions.

You will feel good about who you are.

By Laura Greco, Parenting Coach

Attention Dads:
Learn to Be Confidently Vulnerable

In my decade-long work with parents of children with either ADHD or Autism Spectrum challenges, I often must help both parent and child learn to embrace their individual vulnerability in order to ask for and receive the help they need.

What I've found is that fathers in our culture can have a really hard time with this idea. They consider it a form of weakness, an insult to their understanding of what it means to be a man.

I've found success in helping them break through this thinking by beginning with the following question: "How do you define vulnerability?"

Responses I received included:

- Failure

- Weakness

- Wimp

- Too emotional

- Open to attack

I wouldn't want to be vulnerable either if this is what it meant. But when it comes to relationships with those closest to us (e.g., our wives and children), vulnerability is key to helping them connect on a deeper level with us as well as to themselves. Most importantly, it teaches our children how to work through their emotions in the service of others without expecting anything in return while developing emotional intelligence, empathy, and resilience. It's through modeling our own vulnerability that our children learn this best.

One of my strengths as a clinician is how vulnerable I'm willing to be with my clients. What compels me and allows me to do this is how I define vulnerability. For me, vulnerability is about showing up in a fully human way and inviting you to join me in that space. In this way, being vulnerable is taking a leadership role instead of a submissive one. To be fully human is to embrace your imperfections, not pretending you have it all together. You're showing up with another human being and acknowledging you share a similar journey in trying to make sense of the human condition. You show up from that very vulnerable, fully human place, modeling it to other people and inviting them to join you there with the promise they'll be safe with you.

To open yourself up in that way for the benefit of someone else is a sign of great leadership and strength. In that moment with you, others learn what a powerful place vulnerability is. They learn what it feels like to be with another person, exactly as they are, without judgment. What a profound gift that is.

Easier said than done, isn't it? The next step is to learn to open your own heart so you can be the vulnerable leader your family looks to you to be. To help you in your journey, I offer the following questions for your reflection:

- How must I define vulnerability to feel strong while expressing it?
- Who in my life allows me to be fully vulnerable and safe with them?
- What do they do or say that I can begin to model?
- Who can I go to for support as I explore being more vulnerable?
- What one thing can I do to begin being more vulnerable with others?

By Brian King, LCSW

Inspiration

Messy Home, Messy Mind

"If a home doesn't make sense, nothing does." —Henrietta Ripperger

I just came across this quote, and it made me stop and think about how true this is; messy rooms, dirty dishes, chaos in our junk drawers, and unplanned meals can certainly have a major impact on each day of our lives. I know for me, if I don't have some order in my home, my mind feels messy too. Actually, some would say that a messy or chaotic outer environment is really just a reflection of the inner state of our beings. I've found that putting the outside in order can also have a reciprocal effect on the inner me.

This all made me think about the systems that I have created over the years and about how implementing those systems in my life while my kids were growing up provided me with a clear mind and wonderful memories. We didn't fight about messy rooms, money, curfews, and homework because I had a system for each of those. Consider implementing the following for a healthy home and healthy mind:

- Regular shopping trips
- Regular bedtimes
- Regular mealtimes
- Regular cleaning days
- Regular laundry days
- Menus for the week
- Schedules for watching TV/using the internet
- Allowances
- Homework time

The key is regularity and schedules! These provided my kids and me the structure we needed for our busy, full, productive lives.

Inspiration

Rainy Day Tool Kit:
Expressive Arts for Creative Minds

Well, it is cold, really cold, and rainy—the kind of day during which you don't want to leave the house. But you know if you don't get out, by the end of the day, your nerves are going to be fried (from your children's fighting and bickering, from their nagging you, from you nagging them), and the kids will have probably lost every toy and privilege under the sun. Those long, sad faces will be looking at you for the rest of the day.

You have probably tried letting them watch TV for hours, but after awhile, as you watch them turn into zombies in front of your very eyes, the guilt gets to you. On one hand, you realize that sitting in front of a talking box just isn't healthy; however, you are out of ideas about what to do. Why can't they just play alone, or together, or just occupy themselves? I'll tell you why.

The kids are out of ideas, just like you are. They are accustomed to using TV, video games, and time on the computer as their wind-down activity. Very rarely do our kids have a whole day of nothingness stretching out before them.

- They need you to provide structure and ideas.
- They need you to spark their creative minds.
- They need you to turn off the TV so they can think and learn and build.

The following are some creative ideas you can pull together in no time with items found around your home:

Play-Doh: Making Play-Doh is super easy. Let the kids make a mess, and once it dries, it is a breeze to clean up. Here is an easy recipe:

- 2 cups flour
- 3 tbsp. cream of tartar
- ½ cup salt
- 4 tbsp. oil
- ½ cup boiling water
- food coloring

Mix dry ingredients together. Mix oil, food coloring, and boiling water in a separate container. Stir liquid mixture and then combine with dry ingredients. Once cool enough, knead until smooth.

If the Play-Doh is too dry, add more water, a little at a time. If the Play-Doh is too crumbly, knead in a small amount of oil. Store in an airtight container.

More ideas:

- **Treasure Chest Shoeboxes:** Magazines and glue sticks are all that is needed to make great art projects. Let kids decorate the boxes and then use them for storing their treasures.

- **Family Photo Gallery:** Go through photographs. Let the kids cut them up and make a collage from the photos from a family vacation.

- **Let's Play School:** Set up a classroom and let the kids be the teachers to each other.

- **Let's Find It!** Have an indoor scavenger hunt.

- **Picnic:** Have a picnic lunch in the family room; sit on beach towels and eat in your bathing suits to mix things up.

- **Fort:** Let the kids build a fort out of chairs and blankets.

- **Performance:** Give your kids a bag of objects and have them put on a skit for you using the objects.

Sit back and watch your kids have fun while knowing that you are sparking their creative minds!

Activity

Parent/Child Boundaries: Access Tokens

Ages: 4–6

Purpose: To help children self-monitor their interactions with an adult, especially when the adult is busy with something.

For young kids, it is sometimes difficult to understand that we parents are not always completely available to them and to their needs. Even when we explain that we need time to work or cook dinner and that they should stay for a while with their dad, older sibling, or babysitter, they don't always grasp that easily and keep interrupting us in what we are doing.

Materials:

- Cardboard
- Scissors
- Glue
- Tokens template below

Instructions:

1. Make a set of three tokens. You can use the tokens below and glue them on a piece of cardboard, or make your own.

2. Whenever you need to attend to a task, such as work, a household chore, or just having some "me" time (knowing that your child is safe with someone looking after them), give them the three tokens and explain to them that this allows them to come see you for any reason they wish.

3. When they come, they need to give you one token; and when they run out of tokens, they cannot come see you anymore unless it is something really, really important like being hurt.

4. You can adjust the amount of tokens you give them to the time you need and/or to the age of the child.

By Priscille d'Arifat-Koenig, Parenting Coach

Inspiration

Free Time? What's That?
Taking Care of You

Whether you are a parent, a professional, or both, it is essential that you recharge your own battery. Throughout this book, I have stressed being "on" with your kids and not allowing their negative behaviors to go unnoticed. I also realize that you require downtime and grownup time.

Making time for yourself while raising kids and/or working with kids can be a huge challenge. In fact, it may feel like an impossibility given your job, long commute, household chores, kids' activities, laundry, meal prep, shopping, cleaning—tired yet?

So where do you fit in eating right, exercising, socializing, alone time, reflection, fun, or just plain doing nothing? Today I want you to do some research; that means keep track of what you do and when you do it.

Notice the following things:

- How many times you check your e-mail, your phone, social networking sites, and so on

- How often you get distracted from what you are doing and don't complete the task, only to have to come back to it later and restart

- How often you wing it without planning and create extra work for yourself

- Your bedtime routines and your mealtime routines

Use the following worksheet to identify the daily activities that are time wasters. After you do this, fill in the activities you want to make time for. All of this will save you precious time and create space for you to do nothing, read a book, or just sit back and put those busy feet up!

Creating Time for Me

List activities that are time wasters:

    1. _____

    2. _____

    3. _____

    4. _____

    5. _____

List those activities that you want to fit in:

    1. _____

    2. _____

    3. _____

    4. _____

    5. _____

Now determine which activities you want to fit in that can take the place of the time wasters. Draw lines from the second list to the first connecting those that can be 1 for 1 replacements.

Are there activities that you used to do, but have given up since having children, such as playing a musical instrument, going to the gym, painting, crafts or something else? Revisit your youth and try these activities again. You may find that this fuels you and gives you even more energy to parent from a place of calm and peacefulness.

Inspiration

Time Away From the Kids

Are you so busy with striving for a clean house and home-cooked meals? For exercising daily, eating right, watching your weight, having rewarding employment, having a social life and fulfillment? For being the best mom or dad you can be?

Do you feel something is missing? Are you noticing:

- you and your partner don't spend time together?
- you and your partner are arguing with no resolution?
- you feel that you are letting him or her down?
- you want to add more intimacy and romance in your life?
- you and your partner have a dream, such as going on vacation, and you don't know how to make that happen?
- you have an issue that is causing stress in your relationship (e.g., kid issues, job issues, troubles with infertility, or your relationship with in-laws)?
- you are going through a life transition, such as a new job, a baby, a new romance, a new marriage, your kids growing up and leaving home, having to care for an elderly parent?

Is it time to start paying more attention to your relationship with your partner? "But we both work full-time, and the kids demand all of our attention!" Paying attention to your relationship will put you both at the top of the list, and when you nurture and support each other, everything else will seem much more manageable.

Steps for Caring for Each Other (and Yourself):

- Get a babysitter if you need to and go out once a week. Pick a night and stick to it. It doesn't have to be Saturday! It doesn't matter what you do—you can even go grocery shopping together. Just make it alone time.
- Make a specific time each evening as "off duty." For example, tell the kids, "Bedtime is 8:30 p.m., and we are now on break; no interruptions." Follow through to ensure you and your partner have at least an hour alone each evening.
- Explore activities and hobbies that you have in common. As your kids get older, begin to do these activities together, such as running, tennis, dancing, skiing, photography, or hiking.
- Talk about intimacy and schedule time to be alone and reconnect. Notice when your partner does something kind and comment to him or her about it.
- Get conscious in your relationship and pay attention to what is going on.

These steps are not automatic, and they take planning and organization. But the work is well worth it in the end. Know that some days the laundry just won't get folded, and there might be some dishes in the sink when you wake up in the morning, but sometimes, letting go of some mundane tasks will be a very worthwhile investment!

Enjoying Your Kids While Working From Home

More and more parents are choosing to work from home, which is great news because kids have more access to their parents. However, working from home while raising a family can present challenges that are difficult to handle, such as:

- Setting limits

- Being interrupted

- Balancing work with family life

Tips for Setting Boundaries:

- Make a schedule and stick to it. Whether you work days, afternoons, or evenings, let your family know your hours. You might hang your schedule in the kitchen or on the door to your office. If you must work while your children are home (after school) arrange for a school-aged babysitter to come over to play with the kids a couple of times a week.

- At the end of your workday, turn off your computer, clean your desk, and make a to-do list for tomorrow. Do not answer your work phone or emails after you have closed shop. If you were at the office, you wouldn't know about these messages until the following morning. These small steps help you to walk away and enjoy time with your family.

- If your office also doubles as family space, create boundaries for your papers and files. If the kids are going to use your "work" computer for homework and surfing, teach them to create folders so everyone's documents have a place to be stored. Give the kids clear instructions about what is acceptable to download. This will eliminate you nagging the kids to get off the computer, and you will also be able to have more pleasant interactions with your family.

- Install a separate phone line dedicated solely to your business. This will keep unwanted interruptions from happening and a clear line of communication open for you and your business. If you can afford to, you can also have a separate computer for the family.

- Enlist your school-aged children to help with office tasks that they can handle, such as stamping envelopes, creating a database, or shredding unwanted documents. If you compensate the kids (with either a special activity or payment), they will want to pitch in. You will also be teaching them how important your work is to all your lives.

- If possible, create other work spaces in your office, where your children can do homework and projects while you catch up on your own work. This allows you to spend time with your children while working.

You have made the choice to work from home and your children are fortunate to have you around. Make your time with your kids fun and look for new and creative ways to allow the kids to participate in your business, thereby increasing time they are spending with you.

Inspiration

Does Your Life Have Rhythm?

Think about the world: day and night; the seasons; the tides going in and out; the days, months, and years. Nature has a rhythm and so do we: we are given an order by which we live. How do you use this? Do you have regular bedtimes, mealtimes, relaxation breaks, workdays, and exercise and movement times? Or are your days spent dealing with chaos and fires to which you are continually spontaneously reacting?

If the latter is the case, you are most likely depleted by the end of the day. Structure helps us keep our energy even and plentiful. Chaos leads to disorganization, poor sleep, poor eating habits, and anxiety. And consequently, our relationships suffer.

What if your days and nights were built on a structure that was easy and fun to implement? Would you want to do this?

The following suggestions are ones I have used over the years to help streamline my life and leave time for the stuff that really matters to me:

- When you prepare a dinner, multiply the recipe at least times two. Freeze the unused portions and label them with a date. This gives you a no-cook night. Once you've got the hang of it, you'll only have to cook a couple of times a week because you'll always have something healthy and tasty that you can defrost, heat up, and serve. (Yippee! More time relaxing and spending time with those you love!)

- Pick a time of day for movement and schedule it on your calendar. (Science is more and more telling us how important regular exercise is not only to our physical health, but to our mental well-being as well.) Do different things each day, such as going up and down the stairs 10 times, taking a short walk around the block, doing a few of your favorite yoga poses, standing at your desk while working, and so on. (Yippee! Even if you don't make it to the gym, you still moved!)

- Pick a bedtime that allows you a minimum of seven hours of sleep. (I plan on nine!) Thirty minutes before bed, turn off the TV, put the laptop, iPad, and phone away, and read a book or a magazine, or do something else that relaxes you and helps you decompress, like taking a bath, meditating, or journaling.

Rhythm has a lot to do with planning. Of course, no matter how much we plan, life happens and things get messy—just like when a hurricane, a blizzard, or an earthquake occurs. But then all settles down and if we have a plan in place before "disaster strikes," it will be much easier to reestablish that rhythm.

Inspiration

What Kids and Cucumbers Have in Common

A few years ago, I planted a vegetable garden with lettuce, pole beans, tomatoes, cucumbers and herbs. Every day I went outside to check it. For weeks very little happened. Then one morning I went out to check again. I couldn't believe my eyes! The tomatoes were three times larger than they were the day before, the lettuce had doubled in size, and the cucumbers had these really cool shoots coming out of them that had actually attached to the fencing and had wrapped around it several times to hold on. My garden had exploded with activity, and it seemed to have happened overnight.

The magic in my garden made me think about my own kids. They used to be little, and then one day—and I can't tell you when—like the shoots of the cucumbers, they were taller than me, were independent, had parts of their lives that didn't include me … and then they were transformed into grownups.

The minutes, hours, days, months, and years flew by in a flash. I have photos documenting that the time spent together actually happened. I remember some of it in bits and pieces, and then some of it is a complete blur.

Looking back, I know that I had spent time looking in their eyes, talking to them, and creating memories every chance I could. What I have today is a wonderful, close relationship with both of them.

You've heard it over and over: "Enjoy them now because when you least expect it, in the blink of an eye, they'll be adults and on their own."

Start by looking into your kid's eyes five times a day. Don't take your eyes off them. Maybe, just maybe, you'll see the magic happening right in front of you.

Bibliography

Barkley, R.A., & Benton, C. (2013). *Your defiant child, second edition: Eight steps to better behavior.* New York, NY: The Guilford Press.

Bradbury, T., & Greaves, J. (2009). *Emotional Intelligence* 2.0. Har/Dol En edition. San Diego, CA: TalentSmart.

Bronson, P., & Merryman, A. (2009). *Nurtureshock: New thinking about children.* New York, NY: Twelve.

Cardone, G. (2011). *The 10X rule: The only difference between success and failure.* Hoboken, NJ: Wiley.

Crawford, C. (2009). *The highly intuitive child: A guide to understanding and parenting unusually sensitive and empathic children.* Alameda, CA: Hunter House, Inc.

Dilley, J. (2015). *The game is playing your kid.* Minneapolis, MN: Bascom Hill Publishing.

Epstein, S. (2007). *Taking back your parenting power system: How to get control of your kids in 30 days or less: The secret formula to powerful parenting.* New London, CT: Shining Star Publishing.

Epstein, S. (2008). *Are you tired of nagging? Get your kids to cooperate: How to raise well-behaved children.* New London, CT: Shining Star Publishing.

Epstein, S. (2012). *Over 60 techniques, activities & worksheets for challenging children & adolescents.* Eau Claire, WI: Premier Publishing & Media.

Epstein, S., & Rosenkrantz, D. (2010). *Your out of control teen: The little book with a lot of attitude: A guide to effective parent-teen communication.* New London, CT: Shining Star Publishing.

Freeman, J., Epston, D., & Lobovits, D. (1997). Stories of hope. In *Playful approaches to serious problems: Narrative therapy with children and their families.* New York, NY: Norton.

Garland, T. (2014). *Self-regulation interventions and strategies: Keeping the body, mind & emotions on task in children with autism, ADHD or sensory disorders.* Eau Claire, WI: Premier Publishing & Media.

Ginsburg, K.R. (2002). *"But I'm almost 13!": An action plan for raising a responsible adolescent.* New York, NY: Contemporary Books.

Ginsburg, K.R. (2006). *A parent's guide to building resilience in children and teens: Giving your child roots and wings.* Elk Grove Village, IL: American Academy of Pediatrics.

Glasser, W. (1998). *Choice theory: A new psychology of personal freedom.* New York, NY: HarperCollins Publishers, Inc.

Godin, S. (2011). *We are all weird.* New York, NY: The Domino Project.

Greene, R.W., & Ablon, J.S. (2006). *Treating explosive kids: The collaborative problem-solving approach.* New York, NY: The Guilford Press.

Hall, K. (2009). *Aspire: Discovering your purpose through the power of words.* New York, NY: William Morrow.

James, B. (1989). *Treating traumatized children: New insights and creative interventions.* New York, NY: The Free Press.

Kindlon, D., & Thompson, M. (1999). *Raising Cain: Protecting the emotional life of boys.* New York, NY: Ballantine Books.

Lowndes, L. (2003). *How to talk to anyone: 92 little tricks for big success in relationships.* New York, NY: McGraw Hill.

Minuchin, S. (1974). *Families and family therapy.* Cambridge, MA: Harvard University Press.

Minuchin, S., & Fishman, H.C. (2002). *Family therapy techniques.* Cambridge, MA: Harvard University Press.

Palmer, S. (2006). *Toxic childhood: How the modern world is damaging our children and what we can do about it.* Great Britain: Orion.

Parry, A., & Doan, R.E. (1994). *Stories re-visions: Narrative therapy in postmodern world.* New York, NY: The Guilford Press.

Pink, D.H. (2005). *A whole new mind.* New York, NY: Riverhead Books.

Pink, D.H. (2011). *Drive: The surprising truth about what motivates us.* New York, NY: Riverhead Books.

Pink, D.H. (2018). *When: The scientific secrets of perfect timing.* New York, NY: Riverhead Books.

Rappaport, L. (2009). *Focusing-oriented art therapy: Accessing the body's wisdom and creative intelligence.* London: Jessica Kingsley Publishers.

Szapocznik, J., Hervis, O.E., & Schwartz, S.J. (2003). Brief Strategic Family Therapy for Adolescent Drug Abuse (NIH Pub. No. 03–4751). *NIDA Therapy Manuals for Drug Addiction, Manual 5.* Rockville, MD: National Institute on Drug Abuse.

Taibbi, R. (2007). *Doing family therapy: Craft and creativity in clinical practice 2nd ed.* New York, NY: The Guilford Press.

Whitworth, L., Kimsey-House, H., & Sandahl, P. (1998). *Co-active coaching: New skills for coaching people toward success in work and life.* Mountain View, CA: Davies-Black Publishing.

Guest Contributors

Gould, Sheryl is a parent coach in Chicago. www.momsoftweensandteens.com

Greco, Laura is a parenting coach who lives in New Jersey. www.ArtofSoulfulParenting.com

Hall, Sandy is a parent coach in Orange County, CA. www.sandyhallcoaching.com

Harris, Courtney, MEd, is a life coach for teens and parents, and a certified positive discipline parent educator. She lives in Austin, Texas. www.courtneyharriscoaching.com

Hill, Myrna, LMFT, is a parenting coach who lives in Washington State. www.powerofwith.com

Jones, Kathyrn is a parenting coach and author of *Step Up. Embrace the Leader Within.* She lives in Adelaide, Australia. www.peacefulparentingsecrets.com

King, Brian, LCSW, is a resilience coach and lives in DeKalb, Illinois. www.MindsetBeforeSkillset.com

d'Arifat-Koenig, Priscille is a school and parenting coach. She lives in Mauritius (a tiny island in the middle of the Indian Ocean!). www.priscillekoenig.com

LaBreque, Karolina, PhD, is a behavior therapist and parenting coach. She lives in Rochester, New Hampshire. www.helptogrowinstitute.com

Mazur, Mindy MPH, is an educational therapist in Milton, Massachusetts.

Perrotti, Wendy is an international coach, author, and speaker who lives in Connecticut. www.wendyperrotti.com

Power, Pamela, MS, is a coach and writer. She recently authored *Max & The Super Dynamos!* and lives in Pittsburgh. www.pamelapowerinspired.com

Rosenkrantz, Daniel is Susan Epstein's son. He lives in Los Angeles.

Shrock, Diane, LMFT, lives in Austin, Texas. www.SimplyShrocking.com

Silverman, Jessica is a parenting coach and consultant as well as an early intervention speech-language pathologist. She lives outside of Philadelphia. www.parentingwithclarity.com

Wilson, Heather E. is the CEO and founder of The Canadian Coach. She lives on Prince Edward Island, Canada. www.thecanadiancoach.ca